Your Unicorn is a Lie

The Myth of Startup Success

Book 1 of the Series

The Startup Conspiracy: What They Won't Tell You

by

Ashutosh Tripathy

Foreword

When Ashutosh approached me to write the foreword for this book, I'll admit, I hesitated. Not because I didn't want to. No, it's because this book, much like the startup world itself, is a brutal slap in the face. But hey, we need that sometimes, right?

I've seen more startups crash and burn than I can count, and I've been around long enough to know why. Hell, I've even been part of a few of those train wrecks myself. The truth is, the startup game today isn't about building something that lasts—it's about looking good while the whole thing burns to the ground. And if you've been in the industry as long as I have, you've probably caught on to this twisted game too.

Ashutosh gets it. This book isn't just a critique—it's an autopsy of what's wrong with the startup world today. The billion-dollar valuations, the obsessive chase for unicorn status, the overfunded vanity projects posing as companies... it's all in here, laid out with the kind of wit and cynicism you'll either love or hate, depending on how many delusions you're still clinging to.

And that's why I'm writing this foreword. Not because I'm an old cynic, but because I've been through the grind. I've seen the unicorns, and let me tell you something—most of them are as mythical as the creature they're named after. I've watched founders, with more investor money than sense, burn through cash like it was a birthday candle, all while pretending they were "disrupting industries" when all they were really doing was setting fire to a pile of investor cash.

Genexis Studio, the company I run, has worked with startups from all over the globe. Some of them have thrived, but many, many more have flamed out spectacularly. What you'll read in this book is the reality of the startup world stripped of its Silicon Valley sheen. It's blunt, it's offensive, and it's damn necessary.

To those of you in the trenches, hustling for your next funding round—this book might just be the wake-up call you didn't know you needed. For the rest of you, buckle up. Ashutosh is about to take you on a wild ride through the hype, the hustle, and the harsh reality that is today's startup ecosystem.

Good luck. You're going to need it.

— **Mukesh Kumar**,

CEO, Genexis Studio

Prologue: The Startup Delusion – Welcome to the Circus

Let me tell you a little secret, one the startup world doesn't want you to know: we're all in a giant, VC-funded circus, and the clowns? Well, that's you, dear startup founder. You think you're building the next Facebook, Google, or Amazon? Spoiler alert—you're probably not. But hey, you've got the same glossy smile, the slick pitch deck, and a boatload of investor cash burning a hole in your pocket. You're well on your way to becoming the next "disruptor" of an industry no one asked to be disrupted. Congratulations.

Here's the thing—this game you're playing? It's not about building a profitable business anymore. That's old-school, grandpa stuff. No, today it's all about perception. How good do you look on the outside while your financials rot on the inside? How many funding rounds can you close before anyone notices that your business model is about as solid as a house of cards in a windstorm?

Unicorns? Ha! The modern-day "unicorn" is nothing more than an overhyped, overvalued shell, propped up by investors who are just hoping and praying you don't crash and burn before they can cash out. And you? You're riding this high like a startup cowboy, thinking you're the next big thing. But here's the brutal truth: you're not even close.

You've been sold a dream—the dream that if you just raise enough money, build enough hype, and promise enough "disruption," you'll be the next household name. The reality? You're just another number in a long line of startups destined to fail spectacularly, but hey, at least you'll go down in a blaze of overfunded glory. And isn't that what it's all about these days?

So buckle up, because this ride isn't getting any smoother. In fact, it's probably going to crash. But until then, keep pretending your unsustainable, discount-driven, investor-baiting startup is the future. And don't forget to smile for the cameras while you're at it.

Welcome to the unicorn dream. Now let me show you why it's really just a nightmare.

Table of Content

Preface 13
The Birth of the Unicorn Myth 16
    A Unicorn? Seriously, Grow Up 17
    The Billion-Dollar Wet Dream 22
    The First Startup Wasn't Even Yours, Bro 26
    Early Success Doesn't Mean You're Not Screwed ... 31
    Why Your Unicorn Dreams Are Just Another VC Drug 36
Valuation Games: Smoke, Mirrors, and Hype 41
    The VC Game: Understanding Funding Dynamics 42
    Valuation Mechanics: What Really Matters 50
        Revenue Generation 52
        Market Size 53
        Customer Acquisition Cost (CAC) vs. Lifetime Value (LTV) 55
        Profit Margins 56
        The Broader Picture 57
    Manipulating Valuations: Smoke and Mirrors 58
    Growth-at-All-Costs Mentality 69
    Consequences of Inflated Valuations 76
The Ponzi Scheme of Venture Capital 85
    The Exponential Growth Expectation 87

  The Pressure to Raise New Funding.........................94
  The Illusion of Sustainability................................. 98
  Early Investors and Their Exit Strategy................. 102
  The Dangers of a Ponzi-Like Structure.............. 107
Profitability vs. Growth: Why You Can't Have Both.................112
  The Growth Obsession: Ignoring Financial Health............114
  Profitability vs. Growth Metrics............................118
  Case Studies of Profitless Unicorns........................122
  The Pressure to Pivot to Profitability....................127
  Long-Term Implications of Growth-Only Focus................. 135
The Cult of the Founder..141
  The Founder's Role: Driving the Hype.............. 142
  Crafting Founder Stories for Investment............. 151
  The Idolization of Founders...................................154
  When the Cult of the Founder Fails.......................159
  Lessons Learned from Founder Failures............. 163
The Customer Acquisition Trap: Discounting to Death...........167
  Discounting as a Strategy: Short-Term Gains...................... 169
  The Pitfalls of a Discount-Driven Market.....................176
  The Challenge of Building Customer Loyalty....................186
  The Long-Term Effects of Constant Discounting.............191
  Case Studies of Companies That Failed.............................196
The IPO Mirage: Going Public Without Profits....................... 201

- IPOs: The Illusion of Success 203
- The Rush to Go Public 209
- Post-IPO Struggles: A Harsh Reality 212
- Case Studies of Failed IPOs 216
- Future of IPOs in the Startup Ecosystem 220
- Investor Exodus: When the Funding Dries Up 224
  - The Importance of Continuous Funding 226
  - Signs of Investor Fatigue 229
  - Consequences of Funding Dry-Up 233
  - Strategies for Securing Additional Capital 237
    1. Revising the Valuation Narrative 237
    2. Desperate Discounting and Promotions 238
    3. Reaching Out to Existing Investors 239
    4. Revising the Pitch Deck 240
    5. Seeking Out New Investors with a Fresh Spin 241
    6. Leveraging Strategic Partnerships 242
    - Conclusion 242
  - Resilience in the Face of Funding Challenges 243
- The Future of Startups: Is There a Way Out? 248
  - Is the Unicorn Model Dead? 250
  - How Stakeholders Can Push for Change 257
  - The Role of Investors in a Healthier Ecosystem 260
- End Note: Vision for a Sustainable Startup Future 265

Preface

Welcome to a reality check—one you might not be ready for, but definitely need. As you flip through the pages of this book, don't expect the usual startup jargon filled with optimism, "disruption," and unicorn fantasies. Instead, prepare yourself for an unfiltered look at the absurd circus that the startup ecosystem has become.

In today's world, being a startup founder is like being a contestant on a reality show where the prize is a billion-dollar valuation, and the stakes are your sanity, integrity, and possibly your investors' trust. It's a game that's rigged, and if you're not careful, you might just find yourself as the punchline in a joke that no one else finds funny.

This book isn't just another collection of feel-good stories about entrepreneurs who "made it big" against all odds. No, this is a no-holds-barred exploration of the darker side of startup culture, where valuations soar on the backs of inflated expectations and reality gets kicked to the curb. We're diving into the charades that many founders put on while their companies are slowly sinking.

I'll be brutally honest: many startups today are more about hype than substance. Investors, eager to chase the next shiny object, pour money into ventures that are as fragile as a house of cards. Founders, desperate to maintain appearances, put on a brave face, all while their businesses are built on a shaky foundation of unsustainable growth and discounted services.

Throughout this book, I'll dissect the myths, the delusions, and the outright fabrications that have become the hallmark of modern entrepreneurship. You'll learn why many so-called "unicorns" are nothing more than fairy tales sold to gullible investors, and how the relentless pursuit of quick riches often leads to a slow, painful demise.

I invite you to join me on this journey as we peel back the layers of pretense and reveal the hard truths lurking beneath. It's time to take a good, hard look in the mirror and ask yourself: are you really building a business, or just playing the part in a tragicomedy?

Let's expose the reality together, and in doing so, maybe—just maybe—we'll find a path to creating something meaningful amidst all the chaos.

— **Ashutosh Tripathy**

Founder & CEO, Xplore Growth

The Birth of the Unicorn Myth

Welcome to the magical realm of unicorns, where dreams come true and every startup is one funding round away from a billion-dollar valuation. Sounds familiar? It should—because this is the kind of nonsense that's been drilled into the minds of eager entrepreneurs worldwide. But let's not kid ourselves. While fairytales make for great bedtime stories, in the world of startups, the truth is far less enchanting.

The birth of the unicorn myth is less about magic and more about a collective delusion—a delusion that has clouded the judgment of founders, investors, and anyone with an internet connection. We've become so infatuated with the idea of the unicorn that we've forgotten what it truly means to build a sustainable business. Instead, we're all chasing after sparkles and glitter, thinking that if we can just raise enough cash and get enough attention, we'll somehow be transported to a land of riches and success.

In this chapter, we'll unpack the absurdity of the unicorn myth. We'll explore how it emerged, why it continues to captivate the minds of aspiring entrepreneurs, and the impact it has on the very essence of what it means to run a business. Spoiler alert: it's not pretty.

So, strap in as we dive into the murky waters of inflated valuations, deceptive metrics, and the wild-eyed optimism that defines today's startup culture. It's time to confront the fantasy head-on and expose the reality lurking behind the glittering façade. Welcome to the great unicorn deception—where the only thing truly magical is the art of making nothing look like something.

Let's begin this adventure into the chaotic world of startups, where the line between success and failure is as thin as the paper your pitch deck is printed on. Are you ready? Good. Because the truth is about to get a little uncomfortable.

A Unicorn? Seriously, Grow Up.

Ah, the beloved unicorn—the mythical creature that has become the poster child for startup success. Can we just take a moment to roll our eyes at this absurdity? Seriously, how did we end up here? We've turned a fictional animal into a symbol of achievement, as if slapping a horn on a horse magically transforms it into something special. It's like a collective brain freeze in the entrepreneurial world, where we're all swiping right on billion-dollar valuations like it's some sort of Tinder game, hoping for a match that will finally validate our existence.

Let's break this down. The term "unicorn" was coined by Aileen Lee in 2013 to represent those elusive startups valued at over a billion dollars. But let's be real here: calling your startup a unicorn is just a fancy way of saying, "Look, my startup's imaginary value is so high that even I believe my own hype." It's a dazzling distraction that allows founders to strut around with their heads held high, pretending their inflated valuation is based on solid metrics when, in reality, it's just a glorified guessing game fueled by investor cash and wishful thinking.

Take WeWork, for instance. This coworking space giant was once hailed as a unicorn, boasting a valuation of $47 billion. Founders Adam Neumann and Miguel McKelvey had the audacity to sell the idea that they were redefining the workplace. Spoiler alert: they weren't. Instead, they were racking up losses faster than they could open new locations. Neumann's lavish lifestyle—complete with private jets and a questionable grasp on reality—became a punchline when the company had to face the music. By 2019, WeWork's valuation plummeted to $8 billion, proving that sometimes the unicorn is just a horse in a fancy costume with a bad haircut.

And here's the kicker: this obsession with unicorn status has created a toxic culture where founders are more focused on impressing investors than actually building something meaningful. It's all about the optics—shiny presentations, flashy pitches, and the promise of future growth. But dig a little deeper, and you'll find that many of these so-called unicorns are built on shaky foundations, with business models that are more fantasy than reality. Just because you've managed to snag a few million bucks doesn't mean you're ready for the big leagues. You're just one market dip away from crashing down faster than a poorly executed pitch at a startup competition.

Let's also consider the ridiculous lengths some founders go to in order to maintain this facade. They hire fancy PR firms to spin their stories, curate social media images that depict their lives as glamorous and successful, and engage in a never-ending cycle of funding rounds. Look at Uber and its infamous "growth at all costs" strategy. They expanded globally, often in violation of local laws, all while drumming up valuations that were simply mind-boggling. Remember when Uber was valued at $68 billion? Fast forward a few years, and the reality set in: they were bleeding money, and their business model was rife with ethical dilemmas. The image of a tech-savvy unicorn faded, leaving a tarnished reputation in its wake.

And let's not forget the other glaring issue: the impact this unicorn fever has on the startup landscape itself. Investors, hungry for the next big thing, are more than willing to throw cash at anything that claims to be a unicorn. But in this race to fund the "next unicorn," are we really doing ourselves any favors? It's as if we've decided that throwing money at every half-baked idea is a better investment strategy than taking the time to nurture solid businesses. The outcome? A lot of hype, very little substance, and a whole generation of founders convinced that they're on the path to greatness, when in reality, they're just playing dress-up in a costume that can't possibly withstand the harsh realities of the market.

For example, consider Oyo Rooms. Once a shining star in the Indian startup ecosystem, Oyo skyrocketed to unicorn status with promises of revolutionizing the hospitality industry. But a closer look reveals a different story—one filled with lawsuits, hotel partnerships gone sour, and the realization that the model relied heavily on aggressive expansion rather than sustainable practices. Just like that, the unicorn was exposed as more of a well-dressed pony, and as investor sentiment soured, so did its valuation, dropping from a peak of $10 billion to a mere fraction of that amount.

So, if your lofty goal is to become a "unicorn," congratulations! You're officially chasing fairytales. You've bought into the dream and convinced a few investors to throw money at your failure-to-be. But let me be blunt: this obsession with unicorns is a recipe for disaster. You're not building a sustainable business; you're trying to polish a turd and hoping that investors won't notice. This quest for mythical status has blinded many founders to the real work that goes into building a successful, lasting enterprise.

Let's face it, folks: the unicorn myth is just that—a myth. It's time to grow up and realize that real success doesn't come from inflated valuations or the quest for mythical status. True success is about creating value, building something meaningful, and yes, maybe even turning a profit once in a while. So, put away the glitter and stop chasing that mythical beast. Instead, roll up your sleeves, get your hands dirty, and start focusing on what truly matters: building a business that can withstand the tests of time and market fluctuations. It's time to get back to reality, where the only horn you need is the one that sounds the alarm for the cold, hard truth.

The Billion-Dollar Wet Dream

Ah, the coveted billion-dollar valuation—the holy grail of the startup world. It's the entrepreneur's version of "mine's bigger than yours," and just like those awful "dad bod" T-shirts, it's cringeworthy and largely unnecessary. Let's be real here: this obsession with hitting a billion-dollar valuation is about as useful as an MBA from YouTube. Sure, it sounds impressive, but what the hell does it even mean?

You know what's actually worth a billion dollars? A real, functioning business model, not the pile of investor cash your startup uses as life support. A billion-dollar valuation should signify something substantial—a company that has cracked the code on profitability, sustainability, and genuine market demand. But in reality, it's more like a poorly executed magic trick: "Now you see the value, now you don't." Just because you've managed to snag some VC dollars and show off a shiny spreadsheet doesn't mean you're building anything of value. It just means you've perfected the art of convincing investors to hand over their cash while you live in a fantasy world where unicorns roam free.

Take the infamous case of Theranos, the blood-testing startup that promised to revolutionize healthcare with its magical device that could conduct hundreds of tests with just a drop of blood. Founder Elizabeth Holmes was hailed as a genius, and her company reached a staggering valuation of $9 billion. But guess what? Behind the glitz and glamour, there was nothing but smoke and mirrors. The product didn't work, and when the facade crumbled, so did the company, leaving investors holding the bag and a public left to wonder how they had been so easily duped.

Your billion-dollar valuation is probably as real as those abs you Photoshop in your Tinder pics—nice on paper, garbage in reality. It's a façade, a glittering promise that has little to do with the actual health of your business. The startup ecosystem has become so enamored with these eye-popping numbers that founders forget the fundamental truth: valuations are not a measure of success; they are simply a number thrown around by investors in a desperate attempt to sound relevant in a crowded marketplace.

And here's the harsh truth: just because investors keep throwing money at you doesn't mean you've "made it." It just means you've sold a bigger dream than the next scammer in line. You're luring in gullible investors with the promise of wealth and fame while conveniently ignoring the fact that you're probably one misstep away from crashing and burning. This is a classic case of all bark and no bite.

Take a look at the rideshare industry. Uber, once hailed as a game-changer, amassed a valuation of over $60 billion, but let's not kid ourselves. The company was hemorrhaging money for years, relying on venture capital to maintain the illusion of success. It took a complete overhaul and a change in leadership for Uber to even begin to figure out how to be a profitable entity. Investors are not blind; they see the red flags waving in the wind. But as long as the party keeps rolling, who cares about the actual business model?

And it doesn't stop there. Look at companies like Juicero, which managed to raise $120 million for a juicing machine that squeezed pre-packaged juice bags. Spoiler alert: people found out they could just use their hands to achieve the same result. The company flopped spectacularly, and those billion-dollar dreams turned into a nightmare faster than you could say "overvaluation."

Founders need to snap out of their fantasy land and realize that chasing after a billion-dollar valuation is akin to chasing a mirage in the desert—deceptive and ultimately futile. The reality is that you could have the highest valuation in the world, but if your business model is trash, it won't matter. You'll still be stuck in the desert, lost and confused, while everyone else has moved on to greener pastures.

The key takeaway here is simple: instead of fixating on the allure of billion-dollar valuations, founders should focus on building solid, sustainable businesses. Stop the charade, put your head down, and get to work. Because at the end of the day, a strong business model is what will truly stand the test of time, not some inflated valuation propped up by investors who are all too willing to believe in the latest fairy tale. So, stop chasing the dream and start building something real—before you find yourself on the other end of a devastating reality check.

The First Startup Wasn't Even Yours, Bro

Spoiler alert: you didn't invent anything new. You're just copying some other unicorn's homework. Welcome to the tech world—where founders recycle business ideas like stale memes and have the audacity to act like they just discovered fire. Seriously, let's take a moment to appreciate the sheer lack of originality here.

Founders today prance around like they're breaking new ground, but most are merely riding on the coattails of the early unicorns, desperately trying to cash in on someone else's brilliance. The OGs—like Google and Facebook—were actual innovators who created entirely new paradigms. What are you? A food delivery middleman or a rideshare app? You're like a modern-day alchemist trying to turn base metal into gold while failing to realize you're really just adding sprinkles to last week's expired cupcake. If originality was a person, it would have long since ghosted you and moved on to more promising ventures.

Let's talk about this phenomenon called "disruption." Founders love to throw that word around like confetti at a New Year's party. But let's be honest: you're not "disrupting industries." You're just the "Uber-for-whatever," throwing old ideas in new wrappers and pretending it's revolutionary. Ever heard of the "Airbnb for boats"? Yeah, it's a thing. Because clearly, what the world really needed was to rent out someone's rowboat for a night, just like it needed a million apps that promise to deliver tacos faster than the speed of light. Newsflash: they don't. You might be left staring at your phone while your tacos take a scenic route through the city, only to arrive cold and soggy.

Take a look at companies like Zomato and Swiggy. Are they redefining the dining experience? Nope! They're merely middlemen in the food delivery game, playing the role of an overpriced waiter who doesn't even know how to cook. Their business models hinge on the flimsy promise of convenience while profiting off restaurants and delivery drivers who are both getting the short end of the stick. Sure, they've wrapped the idea of "food delivery" in a shiny app, but what innovation have they brought to the table? It's like putting a new label on a can of beans and calling it gourmet. Spoiler: it's still beans.

And don't get me started on the endless parade of "social media platforms." How many "new" apps have popped up claiming to be the next Facebook or Twitter? You'd think after all this time someone would come up with something original instead of creating yet another platform for people to air their dirty laundry. Each new app launches with a slick marketing campaign, promising to change the world, but it usually ends up as just another digital graveyard of abandoned profiles. "Join us! We're the future!" they cry. No, you're not. You're just another failed Tinder date trying to get a second chance. Remember when Vine was all the rage? The "next big thing" in short video sharing? Now it's a relic, and every new TikTok clone out there has about as much staying power as a paper umbrella in a monsoon.

Even the likes of Oyo, which positioned itself as a hotel disruptor, aren't exactly setting the world on fire with innovation. Sure, they offered budget-friendly accommodations, but are they really changing the landscape of hospitality? Hardly. They're just adding a layer of complexity to a centuries-old business. By the time you realize you've booked a room with them, you're in for a surprise—like the fact that the "five-star" room you paid for doesn't even have hot water. They promise you a luxury experience at a discount, but you end up in a room where the only luxury is that the sheets are almost clean. Talk about an industry "disruption," right?

It's not just Oyo; the entire hospitality sector is drowning in a sea of mediocrity, all while shouting about "disruptive innovation." You can throw a billion dollars at a tired business model, but it doesn't change the fact that most of these companies are just glorified booking agents with a tech-savvy logo. They don't innovate; they imitate, and it shows.

So, what's the key takeaway? Unicorns were once rare and interesting, filled with promise and originality. Now? They're just another Pinterest board of recycled concepts for the "idea-starved" generation. The entire tech scene feels like a never-ending cycle of reboots—like the umpteenth remake of a classic movie that nobody asked for. If originality were currency, many founders would be bankrupt. So before you tout your startup as the next big thing, take a good, hard look in the mirror and ask yourself: Am I really innovating, or am I just rehashing someone else's homework and hoping no one notices?

Let's be clear: being a successful startup founder isn't just about having a cool name and a flashy website. It's about delivering real value and creating something that hasn't been done a thousand times before. But in a world where "disruption" has become a buzzword devoid of meaning, it's no wonder so many startups struggle to find their footing. If you want to create something lasting, it's time to roll up your sleeves and dig deeper than the surface-level gimmicks and trends that define the startup landscape today. Otherwise, you're just another player in a game that's been rigged long before you entered the arena.

Early Success Doesn't Mean You're Not Screwed

Let's set the record straight: just because your startup hit some early milestones doesn't mean you're the next Steve Jobs. Most early successes in startups are as stable as the stock market on April Fool's Day—there's a lot of hype, a lot of noise, and then suddenly, everyone is left wondering what just happened. Congratulations on your temporary success, but remember, early wins are often as useful as a chocolate teapot.

The success that founders celebrate is often just a bump of good PR, not sustainable growth. They hit early revenue targets, start believing their own press, and BAM—they're taking selfies with a rented Tesla, pretending like they're the next big thing. Reality check: just because you've scored a few early wins doesn't mean your business is built to last. In fact, the best way to gauge a startup's potential longevity is to look beyond those early milestones and assess what's lurking beneath the surface.

Take Zomato, for example. In its early days, it was hailed as the golden child of the food tech industry, boasting impressive revenue growth and an expanding user base. Investors were throwing money at it like confetti, and the media couldn't get enough of its supposed "disruption" in the dining space. But fast forward a few years, and the cracks started to show. What was once celebrated as an innovative service became notorious for its razor-thin margins and a customer experience that could best be described as inconsistent at best. Zomato may have had a meteoric rise, but it also faced numerous challenges, including increasing competition and a business model that often seemed to rely on heavy discounting to attract customers—an unsustainable practice that left them scrambling for profitability.

Let's look at Zomato's rollercoaster ride for a second. Its initial growth was fueled by investor enthusiasm and aggressive marketing tactics. The company rapidly expanded its services and geographical footprint, quickly becoming synonymous with food delivery in India. However, this expansion came at a cost. As Zomato grew, so did its operational complexities, and the company struggled to maintain service quality while managing logistics.

The once-coveted app faced severe backlash for delivering cold food, late orders, and poor customer service, leading to public relations nightmares. Zomato's initial success masked the reality of an over-leveraged business model that relied heavily on continuous funding rounds to sustain itself. It wasn't until they were forced to scale back operations and focus on profitability that the true state of the business became evident. Zomato's rocky path serves as a glaring reminder that early success doesn't guarantee longevity; in fact, it can be a false dawn, leading to a rude awakening.

Congrats, you hit $1M in revenue. Now let's see how you handle your next ten years when your business model starts looking like Swiss cheese, full of holes and devoid of any real structure. It's cute to celebrate hitting those revenue targets, but have you thought about what comes next? Spoiler alert: it's a lot of sleepless nights and chasing after elusive profits.

And what about Uber? Initially celebrated for its rapid growth and disruptive business model, it quickly became a global phenomenon. Investors were showering it with money, and the media was in a frenzy. But behind the scenes, it was a different story. Uber was plagued with a myriad of problems, from regulatory issues to internal scandals and a reputation for mistreating its drivers. The company's explosive growth didn't translate into sustainable profitability, and despite all the hype, it was evident that Uber's foundation was shaky at best. Early milestones masked significant operational challenges that would come to haunt the company. What initially seemed like unstoppable momentum turned into a chaotic struggle to remain relevant in an ever-evolving industry.

The reality is that early successes can create a false sense of security. Founders might think they've cracked the code to success, only to find themselves grappling with market saturation, intense competition, and a desperate need for profitability. For every milestone achieved, there are countless hurdles that remain unaddressed.

Let's also talk about WeWork. In its early days, WeWork was the talk of the town. The company was revolutionizing the way people viewed office spaces, and its valuation skyrocketed to nearly $47 billion at its peak. But it turned out that the business model relied heavily on leasing properties long-term while renting them out short-term. This brilliant plan came crashing down when investors realized that WeWork was bleeding money faster than it could fill its spaces. The founder's flamboyant lifestyle and erratic behavior didn't help either, leading to his ousting and a plummet in valuation.

Here's a hard truth: just because your startup is raking in cash doesn't mean you're not one bad quarter away from disaster. That early success could just be a well-timed stroke of luck or a result of a booming market. As the economy fluctuates, the sustainability of your business will be tested, and if you've built your foundation on sand, you're in for a rough ride.

Ultimately, early success can be a double-edged sword. It can fuel your ambition and drive you to push harder, or it can lull you into a false sense of security, making you complacent and unprepared for what's ahead. The key takeaway? Celebrate your wins, but don't let them cloud your judgment. Stay grounded, stay vigilant, and always be prepared for the unexpected.

Why Your Unicorn Dreams Are Just Another VC Drug

Let's face it: VCs are the drug dealers of the startup world, and your startup is just another junkie begging for a fix. The more funding you raise, the deeper you sink into their cycle of dependency, and suddenly you're an overgrown startup with a terminal money burn problem, flailing around and crying for help. It's like a bad relationship—you know it's toxic, but you just can't help yourself because the allure of the cash is too strong.

Let's break this down. When you start out, the idea of unicorn status sounds seductive. Who wouldn't want to be labeled a "unicorn," prancing around with a billion-dollar valuation like you're some kind of tech royalty? But here's the catch: that unicorn status is nothing more than a marketing tool for VCs to keep pumping cash into you. It's their version of a high-stakes casino, where they gamble on shiny new toys, and they don't care if your startup dies in the process—so long as they get their cut. They'll throw money at you faster than a frat boy at a party, but the moment you start to falter, good luck finding them.

Take the case of OYO Rooms. This once-celebrated hospitality startup was touted as the next big thing, disrupting the traditional hotel industry with its innovative model. VCs couldn't get enough of the hype and started pouring money into OYO like it was water in a desert. Sure, the valuation skyrocketed, and the media sang its praises, but behind the scenes, it was a different story. The company struggled with operational inefficiencies, ballooning losses, and a mounting debt crisis. OYO became emblematic of the dangers of VC funding—a tale of excessive cash leading to over-expansion without a sustainable business model. Ultimately, the high-flying unicorn came crashing down, leaving behind a trail of dissatisfied investors and a tarnished reputation.

What does this tell you? VC money is like your shady neighborhood loan shark—keep taking it, and pretty soon you'll find yourself paying interest with your soul. You might think you're in the driver's seat, but in reality, you're just another pawn in their game, set to follow a predetermined script that benefits them far more than it ever will you. You're lulled into believing that every round of funding is a sign of success, when in fact, it's just a way for VCs to maintain their positions of power, feasting on your dreams while you chase that elusive unicorn.

Let's talk about the real winners in this scenario: the venture capitalists. They're the ones cashing in on your hard work, leveraging your potential while you scrape by on scraps. They want you to chase after that billion-dollar valuation because it keeps them in the game. It's all part of the show—where they parade around as if they're helping you achieve your dreams, when in reality, they're holding the strings and pulling you deeper into their web of control.

So here's the bottom line: the unicorn dream isn't a business strategy; it's a VC scam that lets founders think they're in control while they're actually riding a train straight to bankruptcy-ville. You might get a taste of success, but it's only a matter of time before reality kicks in. When that happens, you'll be left holding the bag, staring into the abyss of your poorly constructed business model, wondering where it all went wrong.

It's time to wake up, founders. Don't let the allure of the unicorn status cloud your judgment. If you find yourself chasing after every round of funding, reassess your goals. It's not about how much money you can raise; it's about building a sustainable business that can stand the test of time. Don't let VCs seduce you into believing that their money equates to success—because the truth is, it doesn't. You need to have a solid foundation, a real business model, and a plan for the long haul.

Instead of playing their game, focus on creating real value. Your startup shouldn't be another pawn in their high-stakes gamble; it should be a self-sustaining entity that thrives on its own merits.

Otherwise, you'll find yourself perpetually in debt, relying on a cycle of funding that will only lead to your demise. In the end, being a unicorn isn't worth the price of your soul.

Valuation Games: Smoke, Mirrors, and Hype

Welcome to Chapter 2, where we dive into the murky waters of startup valuations—a landscape that makes your average carnival game look like a walk in the park. Here, we unravel the smoke and mirrors behind the dizzying figures that get tossed around like confetti at a New Year's bash.

Ever notice how every startup seems to have a valuation that's skyrocketing faster than a SpaceX rocket? It's like watching a magician pull rabbits out of hats, except instead of rabbits, we're pulling inflated numbers out of thin air. One minute you're worth $10 million, and the next, thanks to a round of funding and some enthusiastic investor speculation, you're a billion-dollar unicorn.

But let's not kid ourselves. This isn't about real business performance. It's about mastering the art of illusion. Valuations are often little more than a product of hype, buzzwords, and a few well-placed tweets from influential investors. Remember, in the startup world, it's not what you've built; it's what you can convince people you've built.

In this chapter, we'll peel back the layers to expose how venture capitalists (VCs) play their valuation games, using funding rounds to pump up numbers and how this ultimately leads to unsustainable growth models. We'll explore the mechanisms behind these inflated valuations, the relentless pressure to grow at all costs, and why the whole charade is often more precarious than it seems. So buckle up—this isn't just a ride; it's a roller coaster of illusions, dreams, and a reality check waiting to happen.

The VC Game: Understanding Funding Dynamics

Let's kick things off by taking a closer look at the VC game—the intricate dance between startups and venture capitalists that resembles a high-stakes poker game more than a legitimate business relationship. Picture this: you're at a fancy gala, your startup is the glittering centerpiece, and the VCs are the well-dressed sharks circling the punch bowl, ready to take a bite. But hold on—before you let those dollar signs dazzle you, let's break down how this funding circus operates.

First off, venture capital is not some altruistic benefactor showering your startup with love and cash because they believe in your vision. Nope, it's more like a business arrangement where VCs expect hefty returns on their investment within a short timeframe. They're looking for the next big win, and if your startup fits the bill, congratulations! You're in the club. But that's only half the story.

Now, how does this all play out? It typically begins with the early rounds of funding—seed and Series A, where the numbers are modest but still impressive enough to get everyone's attention. At this stage, you're not just selling your business; you're selling a dream, a vision of what could be. You polish your pitch deck until it shines, sprinkle in some buzzwords, and make your projections look as juicy as possible.

Here's where the game gets interesting. Investors, enamored by your potential, start throwing money at you like confetti. But this isn't a charity; they want something in return. The moment you accept their cash, you enter a contract—sometimes even a moral one—that you'll deliver results. And that's where the pressure begins.

Once you secure that funding, it's time to grow, grow, grow. There's a constant expectation for your startup to scale at an alarming rate, which often leads to reckless spending. This can mean ramping up marketing efforts, hiring new talent, or expanding operations—anything to show those glowing metrics that investors crave. And guess what? The more you grow, the more your valuation skyrockets. It's a never-ending loop of raising funds, inflating numbers, and hoping like hell that you don't crash and burn before the next funding round.

But here's the catch: while it might seem like you're swimming in a pool of cash, the reality is that this money is not really yours. It's more like a ticking time bomb. You're under constant scrutiny, and every quarter you're expected to deliver jaw-dropping numbers. If you don't? Well, let's just say that those happy investors can turn into frenzied critics faster than you can say "burn rate."

In the end, the VC game is a delicate balancing act. It's a world where perceived value often trumps actual performance, and startups find themselves in a hamster wheel of growth, running faster and faster just to stay in place. So while you're out there charming investors with your sparkling personality and grand visions, just remember: the money isn't free, and the stakes are as high as they come.

Now that we've covered the game itself, let's talk about the actual process of how valuations get decided—or should I say, how they often get manipulated. You might think that a startup's worth is determined by cold, hard metrics, but in reality, it's more akin to a high school popularity contest where the "cool kids" (i.e., the investors) get to decide who's in and who's out.

Valuations are often set during funding rounds, but they're not based solely on revenue or profits—far from it. Instead, they rely heavily on projections, market potential, and yes, the buzz surrounding the startup. If you have a compelling story and a glitzy pitch deck, you might find your valuation inflated beyond belief. It's all about narrative; if you can tell a good enough story, even the most absurd number might seem plausible.

For instance, take the infamous case of WeWork. At its peak, the company was valued at a staggering $47 billion—despite never turning a profit. How did they get there? It was a combination of aggressive marketing, a charming founder (who, let's face it, was a bit of a showman), and a hell of a lot of hype. Investors bought into the narrative that WeWork was revolutionizing the way we think about workspaces, leading to sky-high valuations that made everyone feel warm and fuzzy inside. But when reality hit, the bubble burst, and that $47 billion dream turned into a $10 billion nightmare.

This leads us to the dark art of valuation manipulation. Startups often play with numbers to make their growth seem more impressive than it actually is. They might strategically time their funding rounds to coincide with favorable metrics or use accounting tricks to present a rosy picture. It's like putting a fresh coat of paint on a rickety old house—it might look good from the outside, but underneath, it's crumbling.

And let's not forget about the role of comparables in this game. VCs often look at similar startups to gauge how much to value a new company. If a competitor just raised a round at a high valuation, you can bet your last dollar that other investors will want to do the same for you, regardless of your actual performance. Suddenly, inflated valuations become the norm, and startups are left chasing that ever-elusive billion-dollar unicorn status without any real foundation to support it.

So while founders might revel in the high valuations thrown their way, the reality is often a house of cards waiting to collapse. When the hype dies down, and the dust settles, those inflated numbers can feel as real as a unicorn prancing through a rainbow. In the end, founders must ask themselves: is this the value we truly deserve, or are we just playing a game of make-believe?

Now let's get real about the problem of growth-at-all-costs. This mentality has taken over the startup landscape like a viral meme, and honestly, it's time we put it to bed. In the quest for that shiny unicorn status, many founders forget a crucial element: sustainability. Instead, they're trapped in an endless chase, burning cash like it's going out of style, all in the name of growth.

Why does this happen? Well, there's a seductive allure to growth metrics. Investors love seeing those numbers rise, and startups often feel immense pressure to deliver jaw-dropping figures, even if it means sacrificing long-term viability. The mantra becomes: grow now, figure it out later. But spoiler alert: this rarely works out.

Take the case of Uber, which famously prioritized growth over everything else. The company threw money at drivers and promotions to corner the market, but at what cost? They were burning billions while never really establishing a profitable business model. The focus on hyper-growth led to a series of scandals, regulatory challenges, and public relations disasters that tainted their brand image. Now, as they scramble to find profitability, that once-stellar growth doesn't seem so appealing anymore.

The reality is that this relentless chase for growth can leave startups with little to show for their efforts. Many end up in a position where they can't sustain their operations without constant influxes of cash. It's like a hamster running on a wheel—lots of movement but not going anywhere fast.

And let's not forget the emotional toll this takes on founders and employees. When growth becomes the sole metric of success, everything else is sidelined. Company culture suffers, employees feel undervalued, and before you know it, you're left with a team of burned-out souls. So, while you might be racing toward those inflated valuations, the human cost is often forgotten in the whirlwind.

In the end, the growth-at-all-costs mentality is a dangerous game to play. It may look glamorous on the surface, but beneath that shiny veneer lies a foundation built on shaky ground. Founders need to step back, take a deep breath, and focus on creating sustainable models that can withstand the test of time—because chasing numbers is one thing, but building a real, thriving business is another entirely.

Now that we've explored these segments, stay tuned as we dive deeper into the next aspects of startup valuations and the twisted reality behind them!

Valuation Mechanics: What Really Matters

When it comes to valuation mechanics in the startup world, it's crucial to separate the hype from reality. Valuations are not simply about how much money you can raise or how many investors are knocking at your door. They hinge on a few key factors that truly matter.

Take, for instance, **revenue generation**. A startup can boast about a billion-dollar valuation based on projections and growth rates, but if it's not generating actual revenue, that valuation is more a product of fantasy than reality. Consider **Theranos**, which was valued at $9 billion without any credible revenue stream or a working product. The allure of the technology—blood testing with just a drop of blood—captured the imagination of investors. But when the company fell apart, it became clear that the valuation was more about the narrative than actual performance.

Next, let's talk about **market size**. Investors often look for a large addressable market when valuing a startup. A small startup operating in a niche market may struggle to command a high valuation, regardless of its growth metrics. **Airbnb**, for example, initially faced skepticism from investors who didn't see the potential in short-term rentals. But as they demonstrated their capability to tap into the massive market of travelers seeking unique accommodations, their valuation skyrocketed. The ability to showcase a vast market opportunity can make a significant difference in how investors perceive value.

Another critical aspect is **customer acquisition cost (CAC)** versus **lifetime value (LTV)**. If a startup spends excessively to acquire customers without a solid plan for retention and maximizing LTV, its valuation can be misleading. **Blue Apron**, the meal kit delivery service, attracted plenty of investment due to its rapid growth, but it ultimately struggled with high customer churn rates. Investors eventually realized that the cost of acquiring customers was unsustainable compared to the revenue generated from those customers. The result? Blue Apron's valuation plummeted post-IPO.

Lastly, let's not forget **profit margins**. A high valuation doesn't mean much if the startup's operating costs are eating away at profits. For example, **WeWork** had a staggering valuation of $47 billion at its peak, but its business model, which involved heavy leasing costs and operational inefficiencies, meant that profits were often an afterthought. When investors started questioning the sustainability of that model, the company's valuation quickly became a cautionary tale.

In essence, understanding the mechanics behind valuations requires a focus on revenue, market size, customer acquisition, and profit margins. It's about looking beyond the buzz and assessing the fundamentals that truly determine a startup's worth. When these elements align, the valuation can be more than just smoke and mirrors—it can be a reflection of a solid business poised for success.

Let's dive deeper into the mechanics behind startup valuations and dissect what really matters in establishing a sustainable and credible value.

Revenue Generation

First, let's revisit **revenue generation**. Startups often pitch impressive valuations based on future projections, but the lack of real revenue can paint a misleading picture. **Theranos** serves as a classic example. Founded by Elizabeth Holmes, the company was initially valued at a staggering $9 billion based on the promise of revolutionary blood testing technology. Investors were captivated by the narrative and vision, but they ignored the fact that the company's actual revenue was negligible and its product was never commercially viable. When the truth came to light, it became a monumental example of how a fanciful valuation can crash and burn when reality doesn't match the hype.

Another example is **Juicero**, a startup that raised $120 million to sell a $400 juicing machine that turned out to be completely unnecessary. Customers could achieve the same results by hand-squeezing juice packs. Juicero's valuation relied on the tech-fueled frenzy but was ultimately a mirage. It's a stark reminder that without genuine revenue, valuations are hollow.

Market Size

Next, consider **market size**. The concept of an addressable market is crucial for investors. If your startup operates in a tiny niche, it's challenging to achieve a high valuation, regardless of how well you perform in that space.

Look at **Slack** as a positive case study. Initially, the team behind Slack didn't set out to create a revolutionary communication tool. Instead, they pivoted from a failed gaming startup to a collaborative platform for teams. They quickly recognized that their target market was expansive—any organization that required communication tools. As they demonstrated the ability to penetrate that massive market, their valuation surged.

Conversely, a small startup with an innovative product might struggle to gain traction if it doesn't tap into a sizable market. **Quibi**, a short-form video platform that raised nearly $2 billion, focused on a very narrow segment—smartphone users seeking bite-sized entertainment. However, they underestimated the competition from established players like Netflix and YouTube, leading to their ultimate demise. Investors were left questioning how a billion-dollar valuation was justified when the addressable market was neither large enough nor differentiated enough.

Customer Acquisition Cost (CAC) vs. Lifetime Value (LTV)

Another crucial aspect is the relationship between **customer acquisition cost (CAC)** and **lifetime value (LTV)**. This metric is pivotal because it tells investors whether the business model is sustainable in the long run.

Let's take **Blue Apron**, which was initially hailed as a game-changer in the meal kit industry. The startup enjoyed explosive growth and attracted significant investment, boasting a valuation of around $2 billion at one point. However, as they spent heavily on marketing to attract customers, they began to experience high churn rates. The cost of acquiring customers was not translating into sustained revenue, leading to a scenario where their CAC far exceeded the LTV. As investors started digging into these numbers, Blue Apron's valuation began to crumble, ultimately falling below its IPO price.

In contrast, companies that maintain a healthy ratio of LTV to CAC tend to sustain their valuations. For instance, **Shopify** offers tools for e-commerce businesses, successfully acquiring customers at reasonable costs while ensuring that their LTV was substantially higher. This balance allowed Shopify to continuously raise their valuation based on solid financial metrics, resulting in market confidence.

Profit Margins

Now, let's delve into **profit margins**. It's one thing to boast a billion-dollar valuation, but what does that mean if the startup is hemorrhaging cash?

Take **WeWork**, which had an astronomical valuation of $47 billion at its peak. The company's business model involved leasing large office spaces and then renting them out, but it was riddled with inefficiencies and unsustainable costs. When the company attempted to go public, the truth about its staggering losses and negative profit margins became evident. Investors who had initially been blinded by the hype started pulling back, and WeWork's valuation collapsed to less than

$10 billion in a matter of months. The downfall served as a harsh lesson on the importance of scrutinizing profit margins and operational efficiency.

In contrast, **Costco** operates on a different model. They sell membership-based access to their warehouse stores, providing bulk products at lower prices. Their profit margins may not be as eye-popping as tech startups, but they have a steady revenue stream and loyal customers that ensure their sustainability. Investors recognize that Costco's solid business model and healthy profit margins are far more valuable in the long run than inflated valuations without substance.

The Broader Picture

In conclusion, the mechanics behind startup valuations boil down to revenue generation, market size, customer acquisition costs, lifetime value, and profit margins. By focusing on these elements rather than just the headline-grabbing valuations, startups can establish a more credible foundation for long-term success. When investors look beyond the hype and examine these core metrics, the true value of a startup becomes clearer. The reality is that valuations should be based on tangible business performance and a viable path toward profitability rather than a fairy tale spun by founders.

As we move forward, it's essential for startups to navigate these valuation waters wisely, keeping a realistic perspective on their worth. This understanding will help them cultivate sustainable growth and avoid the pitfalls of chasing inflated valuations that often lead to disaster. So, if you're a founder caught up in the excitement of unicorn status, take a moment to assess the real mechanics behind your valuation—it might just save you from riding the rollercoaster of false expectations.

Manipulating Valuations: Smoke and Mirrors

Oh boy, let's dive into the wild world of manipulating valuations, shall we? Grab your popcorn, folks, because this is a ride through the smoky mirrors of startup land where the only thing more inflated than a unicorn's ego is its valuation.

Imagine you're at a carnival, right? You stroll past the stalls, your eyes glittering with hope and sugary cotton candy, when suddenly you spot a booth labeled **"Get Your Startup Valuation Here!"** You walk up, and what do you find? A magician in a top hat, pulling rabbits out of a hat while simultaneously showing you how to pull numbers out of thin air. Welcome to the magical realm of startup valuations, where the reality is murkier than a swamp monster's bathwater.

Let's set the scene: you're a fresh-faced entrepreneur, brimming with ideas. You've built a product that, if we're being honest, might not even serve a purpose other than to take up space on someone's desk. But no matter! You've got dreams bigger than a house and a pitch deck that could dazzle even the most cynical investor. You raise your first round of funding and voila! Your valuation is suddenly skyrocketing like Elon Musk after a Red Bull. But here's the kicker: your startup is valued at, oh, let's say, $10 million. Why? Well, because your mother told you you're special, and a few well-placed buzzwords like "disruption," "synergy," and "blockchain" go a long way in fooling investors.

Take **WeWork**, for instance. It was the golden child of the startup world, claiming a whopping valuation of $47 billion. They told investors they were changing the way people work. In reality, they were just renting office space like a landlord with an attitude problem. The whole operation was akin to that friend who claims to be an artist while they're really just selling paintings of ducks. "Look, everyone loves ducks!" They thought they were the next Picasso, but we all know they were just a quack away from disaster. Spoiler alert: when WeWork went public, the truth emerged like a bad haircut in a high school yearbook photo. Their financials were about as appealing as week-old sushi, and their valuation collapsed faster than a house of cards in a windstorm.

Now let's talk about the magical game of **creative accounting**. This is where the real fun begins! Imagine if you could just make money disappear. Wait, you can! Just ask your accountant. With some dazzling footwork, you can juggle your expenses and revenues until they look like they're in a Cirque du Soleil performance. You might take a page from the **Theranos** playbook, where they claimed their machines could perform all sorts of medical miracles with a single drop of blood. The reality? Their technology was as effective as using a Magic 8-Ball for medical diagnoses. But hey, their valuation soared to $9 billion because who wouldn't want to invest in the next best thing, right? Until the magic wore off, and suddenly investors realized they were left holding a bag of broken promises.

And speaking of promises, let's discuss the art of **overestimating growth potential**. You know that friend who claims they'll lose 20 pounds in a week but can barely lift a dumbbell? Yeah, startups are just like that! Every founder thinks their product is going to take over the universe, and with a sprinkle of wishful thinking, they start to present growth projections that could make even the most seasoned fortune teller raise an eyebrow. **Juicero** is the prime example of this. They raised $120 million to sell a $400 juicer that you could operate with a smartphone app. Let that sink in. They sold people on the idea that juice was somehow enhanced by Wi-Fi. Spoiler alert: you could just squeeze the bag of juice with your hands and save yourself the cash. But hey, let's pump up that valuation!

Of course, we can't forget the **illusion of market demand**. Picture this: your startup launches a product, and you're convinced everyone on the planet needs it. Meanwhile, the reality is that only your grandma and her knitting circle are interested. But don't let that deter you! You can hire a fancy marketing team that creates buzz so loud that it echoes through the startup universe. You pump out press releases like they're going out of style and throw around terms like "disruptive technology" until people believe your product is the next iPhone. Just ask **Quibi**, the short-form video app that spent $2 billion to lure in users with celebrity content. They had all the glitz and glamour, but when the curtain fell, no one was left in the audience. They crashed harder than a toddler learning to ride a bike.

And now, let's touch on **the myth of user engagement**. Your user base is growing! Hooray! You're on top of the world! Or are you? If your app has more downloads than a free weather app but your user engagement is as low as a snail on a lazy day, you've got a problem. But hey, just keep throwing those inflated numbers at potential investors and watch them ooh and aah. Just look at **Blue Apron**, which went public at a valuation of $2 billion. They had tons of customers signing up, but guess what? Those customers weren't sticking around to keep the business afloat. Their model was built on discounting and freebies, so when the time came to pay full price, they vanished faster than your motivation on a Monday morning.

At this point, let's take a quick detour and examine **the role of venture capitalists**. Ah, the VCs—those suave, slick-talking investors who come swooping in like a superhero, but their capes are made of cash. They promise to take your startup to the moon and back, but let's be real, they're often just in it for their own exit strategy. It's like a bad relationship where you think they're in it for love, but they're just looking for the quickest way to cash in. Take **Snapchat**, for example. The company boasted a massive valuation, and the VCs were drooling over it like a kid in a candy store. They kept feeding it cash while pushing for growth that was unsustainable. When Snapchat finally went public, investors quickly realized they were just another social media platform in a saturated market. Valuations came crashing down faster than a college student after a night out.

And let's not forget about **the hype cycle**. Ah, the hype cycle! It's a beautiful thing where ideas soar like eagles only to plummet to earth like lead balloons. The media love to latch onto the newest startup, painting them as the saviors of the industry, the innovators of our time. But how often do you hear about the fall of a company? Rarely. The media want clicks, not the truth. **Kickstarter** projects often go through this cycle. They get all the initial buzz, raising millions based on lofty promises. But when the reality hits and backers don't receive their products, the internet is rife with disappointment.

In this dazzling game of manipulating valuations, the fundamental rule is that **reality often lags far behind expectations**. Your valuation may look great on paper, but if you peel back the layers of smoke and mirrors, you'll often find a hot mess beneath. And let's be real: if you're relying on hype, wishful thinking, and creative accounting, you're essentially playing with fire.

Let's take a look at **Juicero** once again. They launched with all the fanfare of a rockstar, raising over $120 million to sell a $400 juicer that came with subscription bags of pre-cut fruits and veggies. The marketing touted it as a revolutionary product that would change the way you consume juice. The reality? It turned out you could achieve the same results by simply squeezing the juice bag with your hands—no Wi-Fi required. Investors were drawn in by the shiny product and compelling pitch, only to be left flabbergasted when the news broke that their "innovative technology" was nothing more than overpriced kitchenware. Juicero is the perfect case study of how inflated valuations can lead to disillusionment.

Then there's **Pets.com**, which became the poster child for the dot-com bubble. They started with a bang, garnering massive media attention and a valuation that soared into the billions. The concept of selling pet supplies online seemed like a golden idea, and the sock puppet mascot charmed viewers everywhere. However, the reality was a different story. The company burned through cash faster than you can say "doggy treat," and by the time they went public, they had no sustainable business model. When they finally went belly up, investors learned the hard way that a catchy mascot doesn't translate into profit.

Don't forget about **Theranos**, which we already mentioned but deserves another round of applause (or facepalms) for their spectacular downfall. Elizabeth Holmes had the world captivated with the promise of a device that could run multiple tests with a single drop of blood. They raised hundreds of millions and gained a valuation of $9 billion. But once the curtains were drawn back, it was revealed that their technology was more of a fantasy than a reality. Investors were left clutching their wallets, and the once-glamorous unicorn turned into a cautionary tale that will echo in startup circles for decades.

And what about the infamous **Fyre Festival**, the festival that was supposed to be the epitome of luxury? The hype was palpable. Influencers posted dreamy pictures of pristine beaches and gourmet meals, and tickets were sold at prices that could rival a luxury vacation. But when attendees arrived, they were met with disaster: soggy sandwiches, flimsy tents, and a complete lack of organization. The valuation of this festival was based on influencer culture and aspirational living, yet it crumbled in mere days. It's a classic reminder that sometimes the glitziest promises can turn into a festival of failures.

Lastly, let's consider the case of **Blue Apron** again, which thought it could revolutionize home cooking. At one point, the meal kit service was hailed as the next big thing, fetching a valuation of $2 billion upon going public. But as it turned out, the excitement around meal kits quickly fizzled out when customers realized they could save a lot of money and time by just shopping for ingredients themselves. Blue Apron was unable to sustain its growth and ultimately found itself struggling to compete in a saturated market. Their rapid ascent to fame left many investors wondering how they could have possibly missed the glaring cracks in the business model.

In conclusion, while the world of startup valuations may glitter with the allure of success, the underlying truth is that these inflated figures often mask the chaos and unpredictability of real business performance. Just like a magician's trick, it all looks enchanting until you realize it's all smoke and mirrors. The moral of the story? Keep your eyes peeled and don't get swept away by the magic show. In the unpredictable landscape of startups, it's crucial to separate the hype from the hard facts, lest you find yourself in a web of inflated dreams and shattered realities.

So, what's the takeaway? Sure, you can manipulate valuations and strut around like a peacock with your head in the clouds. But when reality comes knocking at your door, it might just be a bill collector looking for payment on all those inflated dreams. Remember, the startup world is a carnival of illusions, and while it's fun to ride the merry-go-round, you might want to keep your feet planted on the ground.

At the end of the day, manipulating valuations might give you a temporary high, but just like any good carnival ride, it's bound to come crashing down sooner or later. So buckle up, because this wild ride of inflated expectations and shattered dreams is far from over!

Growth-at-All-Costs Mentality

The growth-at-all-costs mentality is like that friend who insists on getting a tattoo every time they drink too much. Sure, it's a wild ride at first, but you can bet there's going to be a regretful morning after. Startups have been caught up in this reckless chase for growth as if it were the Holy Grail. The mantra? "We need more users! More revenue! Who cares about profits?" Spoiler alert: it doesn't end well.

Just look at **WeWork**. They went from being a darling of the startup world to a cautionary tale. The company was all about growth, rapidly expanding its footprint and amassing enormous valuations while racking up losses like it was going out of style. They were renting office spaces and then leasing them to startups at a markup, all while burning cash faster than a bonfire at a college party. Their CEO, Adam Neumann, epitomized the growth-at-all-costs mentality, spouting grand visions while his company floundered financially. By the time they attempted an IPO, investors were left wondering how a company with such massive losses could justify its astronomical valuation. The fallout was swift and brutal, leading to Neumann's ousting and a valuation crash that wiped billions off the balance sheet.

Another prime example is **Uber**, which has long chased growth like a dog after a squirrel. They poured money into expanding their service internationally, often ignoring local regulations and competitive landscapes. The result? A string of legal battles and reputational damage that overshadowed their aggressive expansion. Despite being the poster child of the gig economy, Uber never turned a profit for years because their focus was solely on getting bigger and faster. It was only after realizing that they couldn't simply keep burning cash to fuel growth that they began to pivot their strategy and look for a path to profitability.

Then there's **Zynga**, the gaming company that was riding high on the success of games like *FarmVille*. Their aggressive push to maintain that growth led to a rapid expansion, hiring more employees and investing heavily in new games. But when the novelty wore off, players abandoned their titles faster than you can say "microtransaction." Zynga's focus on constant growth without a sustainable model resulted in plummeting stock prices and multiple layoffs. It's a classic case of how trying to ride the growth wave can quickly turn into a wipeout.

The relentless chase for growth also creates a toxic culture within startups, often pushing employees to their breaking points. Take **Tesla**, for example. Elon Musk's obsession with hitting production targets has led to reports of grueling work hours, pressure cooker environments, and high employee turnover. Employees are often seen working 80-hour weeks to meet Musk's lofty production goals, leading to burnout and even safety concerns. While Tesla's growth has been remarkable, it raises the question: at what cost? The mantra of "growth at all costs" can turn a once-promising startup into a breeding ground for disillusionment and exhaustion.

And let's not overlook **Peloton**, which experienced explosive growth during the pandemic. The surge in demand for at-home fitness solutions propelled Peloton into the limelight, leading to hefty investments in marketing and production. However, as the world started to open up again, sales took a nosedive, leaving them with an oversupply of inventory and diminishing returns. Peloton had to pivot quickly, resorting to layoffs and restructuring to save itself from a tailspin. This situation showcases how the growth-at-all-costs mentality can lead to unsustainable business practices that ultimately threaten the very existence of a startup.

In essence, the growth-at-all-costs mentality is like a sugar rush: it may feel good initially, but it leads to a crash that leaves you feeling empty and regretful. Startups must realize that sustainable growth requires a balanced approach, focusing on building a solid foundation and nurturing their business rather than simply chasing the next shiny user metric. Otherwise, they risk finding themselves in a situation where they're left with little more than an unsustainable model and a headache from their reckless pursuit of growth.

Picture this: you're at an all-you-can-eat buffet, and instead of enjoying a well-balanced meal, you're just shoveling food into your mouth like there's a prize at the end. That's essentially what startups are doing when they pursue growth without thinking about the long-term consequences. They're so focused on gobbling up users and revenue that they forget to check if they can actually sustain themselves.

Take **Snapchat**—a prime example of a company that fell into the growth trap. Remember when everyone was raving about Snapchat stories? They had users flocking to the platform faster than moths to a flame. In an attempt to keep that growth rolling, Snapchat introduced new features like *Snap Map* and *Spectacles*, thinking they could diversify their offerings. The problem? Most users were like, "Cool, but I just want to send funny dog filters." Their focus on chasing growth led to a series of half-baked features that confused users and ultimately led to a mass exodus of users to competitors like Instagram. Snapchat's stock tanked, and they found themselves scrambling to re-engage their audience, showcasing how the pressure to keep growing can lead to missteps that alienate the very users you're trying to attract.

And how about **Better.com**? This online mortgage lender had a meteoric rise, fueled by heavy investment and a focus on aggressive growth. But when their CEO, Vishal Garg, decided to lay off 900 employees over a Zoom call, the world got a front-row seat to how that growth-at-all-costs mentality can create a toxic work environment. The backlash was swift and brutal, damaging their reputation and prompting questions about their internal culture and values. Better.com thought they were just growing their user base, but they ended up with a public relations nightmare that could've easily been avoided had they prioritized sustainable growth practices over flashy metrics.

Even **Netflix**, a company that once seemed untouchable, felt the burn of this mentality. In its early days, Netflix focused heavily on growth by acquiring subscribers like there was no tomorrow. They pumped money into producing original content at a breakneck pace, convinced that more content equated to more subscribers. But when subscriber growth plateaued, they found themselves knee-deep in debt with a massive content library that was more of a burden than an asset. Suddenly, they were scrambling to cut costs, raise prices, and manage subscriber churn. Netflix learned the hard way that unchecked growth can lead to a world of hurt—sometimes, less really is more.

And let's not forget about **Wayfair**, the online furniture retailer that shot up in value during the pandemic, largely due to an explosion of online shopping. They were scaling like crazy, but behind the scenes, they were burning cash faster than a pyromaniac at a bonfire. Their strategy relied heavily on marketing and advertising expenses to lure customers, but when the pandemic eased, and people started returning to physical stores, Wayfair faced a sharp decline in sales. They had to pivot from their growth-focused mindset to address sustainability and profitability, leading to layoffs and restructuring efforts.

The bottom line is this: the growth-at-all-costs mentality is like a kid in a candy store—exciting at first, but disastrous in the long run. Startups need to wake up and smell the coffee (preferably a balanced blend, not a triple-shot mocha), realizing that growth should be about building a sustainable, resilient business model rather than just chasing flashy metrics. If they don't, they might just find themselves on a one-way ticket to bankruptcy-ville, sitting next to all those other startups that got too caught up in their own hype.

Consequences of Inflated Valuations

Alright, let's get real about the consequences of inflated valuations because, let's face it, this is where the rubber meets the road, and it's not pretty. Imagine you're walking around with a fake designer handbag, feeling all bougie, only to have it fall apart at the seams. That's pretty much what happens when startups inflate their valuations and then have to face the reality of their financial situation.

First off, one of the most glaring consequences is that **it sets unrealistic expectations**. When a startup boasts a billion-dollar valuation, they suddenly feel like they're sitting on a throne of gold. Founders start to believe they can do no wrong, and investors think they've struck gold. But here's the kicker: this can lead to severe disappointment when they fail to deliver on the hype. Remember the hot mess that was **Theranos**? Valued at $9 billion, it was all smoke and mirrors. Investors were blinded by the promise of revolutionizing healthcare, but in reality, it was just a scam. When the truth came out, it wasn't just the company that fell; it took down investors' reputations and trust in the startup ecosystem.

Then there's the issue of **talent retention**. High valuations can lure top talent in, but what happens when the reality doesn't match the hype? Employees start questioning their job security and the company's sustainability. When **WeWork** hit its inflated valuation of $47 billion, it attracted tons of talent. Fast forward a few years, and after a failed IPO, the company's value plummeted, leading to mass layoffs and a toxic culture that left many employees scrambling for new jobs. When your company's value is built on shaky ground, it's not just investors who get burned—your team does too.

Moreover, inflated valuations can lead to a **culture of entitlement**. If founders start believing their own hype, they may begin to act like they're untouchable. This can manifest in all sorts of disastrous ways—like excessive spending on perks that don't contribute to the business. Just look at **Juicero**, the juice startup that raised $120 million based on the promise of revolutionizing the juicing experience. They had fancy offices and a ridiculously over-engineered juicing machine, but when it turned out you could just squeeze the juice packs with your hands, investors were left scratching their heads. Juicero's inflated valuation turned into a punchline, showcasing how delusions of grandeur can lead to laughable failures.

And let's not forget about the **market's reaction** to these inflated valuations. When a company like **Uber**, valued at around $82 billion, fails to turn a profit, it can shake investor confidence across the board. The moment investors start to realize that these unicorns might just be overpriced ponies, the market can shift dramatically, leading to a reckoning for the entire industry. This is what we call a *market correction*, and it often hits hard, leaving a trail of casualties in its wake.

Ultimately, inflated valuations can create a **disconnect between reality and investor expectations**. When a company fails to live up to its inflated valuation, the fallout can be severe. This includes loss of investor confidence, legal repercussions, and reputational damage that can take years to mend. The IPO market gets jittery, leading to a slowdown in new offerings, as investors become more cautious about what they're willing to back.

So, in essence, inflated valuations can turn into a **double-edged sword**. On one side, they can attract attention, funding, and talent; on the other, they can lead to disillusionment, failure, and a swift trip down the slippery slope of bankruptcy. If founders aren't careful, they might just find that the shiny veneer of their inflated valuation hides a world of chaos underneath. Instead of building empires, they might end up constructing houses of cards—ready to topple at the slightest breeze.

First, we have the **unrealistic expectations** that inflated valuations set. It's akin to stepping into a high-end restaurant with a menu full of items you can't afford, only to find out your wallet is as empty as your hope for a five-star meal. When a startup claims a valuation of, say, $1 billion, it creates a narrative that they're doing something groundbreaking. Founders puff up their chests and start making bold claims about their revolutionary impact on the world.

Take **Robinhood**, for instance. At one point, it was valued at $11.2 billion, riding the wave of the trading app frenzy. Investors were salivating at the idea of democratizing finance. But when they faced regulatory scrutiny and allegations of market manipulation, the valuation came crashing down faster than a poorly placed avocado toast in a hipster café. Suddenly, the lofty expectations collided with harsh realities, leaving investors feeling duped and customers questioning the integrity of the platform.

Then there's the **talent retention issue**. When a startup boasts an inflated valuation, it might attract top talent, but this can be a double-edged sword. Employees initially join for the promise of being part of something revolutionary, only to find themselves navigating a sinking ship. If the company fails to deliver on its hype, it can lead to mass exodus as employees jump ship in search of greener pastures. Look at **Zenefits**, the HR software company that was once valued at $4.5 billion. When it was revealed that the company was cutting corners on licensing, not only did their valuation drop, but they also faced a talent drain as employees fled the sinking ship, disillusioned by the company's lack of integrity.

Now, let's talk about that insidious **culture of entitlement** that inflated valuations can foster. When founders start believing they're untouchable, it can create a toxic environment. Imagine a CEO cruising around in a company-funded luxury car while the employees are stuck in a cubicle with outdated furniture. It breeds resentment and disengagement among the workforce. Just look at **Theranos** again—Elizabeth Holmes surrounded herself with lavish parties and an extravagant lifestyle, all while the core technology was crumbling. This disconnect between the extravagant lifestyle of the executives and the reality of the business led to a toxic culture that was ultimately unsustainable. Employees soon realized they were part of a grand illusion rather than a groundbreaking tech revolution.

Inflated valuations also lead to irrational **spending habits**. Founders can develop a sense of invincibility, thinking, "Hey, we've got a billion-dollar valuation; let's blow a chunk of it on office ping pong tables and espresso machines!" This type of spending can drain resources that should be allocated towards building a sustainable business. Just look at **WeWork**—the lavish office spaces, the free beer on tap, and a culture of excess led to a burn rate that would make even the most reckless spenders blush. When reality hit and investors took a closer look at the numbers, it became evident that the glamorous façade couldn't hold up to scrutiny. WeWork's valuation went from a peak of $47 billion to a meager $8 billion, leading to a fire sale that left many investors scrambling.

And let's not forget about the **market's reaction** to these inflated valuations. Investors are savvy, and when the shiny packaging starts to show signs of wear, they get skittish. The tech market can be more volatile than a teenager's mood swings, and when they realize that these unicorns are, in fact, glorified ponies, it can lead to a market correction. Take **Snap Inc.**, for example. Valued at $24 billion at its IPO, Snap struggled to demonstrate consistent growth and profitability, leading to plummeting stock prices. Investors were quick to realize that behind the colorful filters and disappearing messages lay a company grappling with monetization challenges. The fall from grace was swift, and investors found themselves nursing wounds that would take time to heal.

Let's also address the **disconnect between reality and investor expectations**. When investors invest based on inflated valuations, they often overlook the fundamental aspects of a sustainable business.

They're so dazzled by the potential of a unicorn that they forget to look at the underlying reality. Companies like **Pets.com** and **Webvan** in the early 2000s serve as stark reminders of this disconnect. Both companies had valuations that soared into the stratosphere based on hype rather than solid business models, only to crash and burn spectacularly. Investors rushed in, only to be left holding the bag when the reality of unsustainable business practices came crashing down.

Inflated valuations create a false sense of security for startups, which can lead to catastrophic failures when the market turns against them. When the shiny veneer begins to peel away, founders find themselves scrambling to maintain the illusion. Instead of focusing on building a robust, sustainable business model, they're left chasing the next round of funding to keep their heads above water. The end result? A parade of startups that collapse under the weight of their own inflated egos.

In summary, inflated valuations create a precarious situation where expectations, talent retention, spending habits, market reactions, and reality are all out of sync. The bubble can only inflate for so long before it pops, leaving a trail of disillusionment and failure in its wake.

If founders and investors don't learn to separate the hype from the reality, they might find themselves on a rollercoaster ride to nowhere, where the only thing they'll end up with is a hefty dose of regret and a massive hole in their wallets. So, buckle up, because in this game, the house always wins—unless you're smart enough to realize that inflated valuations aren't the same as real value.

The Ponzi Scheme of Venture Capital

Welcome to the wild and wacky world of venture capital, where the stakes are as high as a kite on a windy day, and the air is thick with a sense of impending doom. If you think venture capital is about nurturing groundbreaking ideas and helping innovators achieve their dreams, think again. It's more like a high-stakes Ponzi scheme where early investors are just waiting for the next round of funding to keep their golden goose alive, all while pretending they're part of something noble.

Picture this: you're at a party, and there's a guy in the corner wearing sunglasses indoors, claiming he's a "visionary" while peddling his latest "revolutionary" app that will change the world. He's surrounded by a gaggle of eager investors, each one convinced that they're about to strike gold. Spoiler alert: they're not. They're just feeding into a cycle of hype, cash burning, and unsustainable expectations that would make even the most reckless gambler raise an eyebrow.

In this chapter, we'll explore how venture capital resembles a Ponzi scheme, where the promise of exponential growth and quick returns leads startups down a rabbit hole of cash burning and dependency. The pressure to raise new funding rounds becomes a game of musical chairs—when the music stops, only a few will be left standing. As the founders chase after the next round of funding, they often lose sight of what really matters: building a sustainable business that doesn't rely on an endless cycle of investor cash.

We'll dive into the expectations that come with venture funding and the detrimental consequences of prioritizing short-term growth over long-term stability. Let's unravel the tangled web of deception and desperation that defines the world of venture capital, where every funding round feels like a temporary fix, masking the underlying issues that could ultimately lead to disaster. Buckle up, because this is going to be a bumpy ride through the depths of startup dependency and the seductive allure of venture capital.

The Exponential Growth Expectation

The grand circus of startup expectations, where exponential growth is the headlining act, and every founder is convinced they're the next ringmaster of success. The pressure is on—investors want growth that looks more like a rocket launch than a gradual ascent. And why wouldn't they? The allure of doubling or tripling revenue overnight is hard to resist, especially when you're holding someone else's money.

But let's get real for a second. Expecting every startup to achieve exponential growth is like expecting every kid in the playground to be the next LeBron James. Sure, some might have the talent and dedication, but the rest? They'll likely trip over their own shoelaces and face-plant into the sandpit. In the world of startups, that's a harsh reality.

Take **WeWork**, for example. The company was hailed as the future of workspaces, growing at an eye-watering rate and attracting billions in investment. But behind that glossy facade was a business model that didn't make sense—heavy spending on lease agreements without sustainable revenue. When investors realized that the unicorn they'd invested in was, in fact, a glorified real estate company with a shiny app, the bubble burst spectacularly. They were left holding the bag while the founders played the "What happened?" card.

And let's not forget **Theranos**, which went from a whisper in the startup world to a billion-dollar valuation faster than you can say "blood testing." The pressure for rapid growth and the promise of revolutionary technology led to a culture of deception. Instead of focusing on actual results, the company built an entire narrative around a product that didn't even exist. It was all about perception over reality, and when the truth came crashing down, it was a harsh wake-up call for everyone involved.

So, why do startups chase this elusive exponential growth? Simple: it's what investors want to see. They're not interested in steady, sustainable progress; they want to see hockey stick graphs that make their eyes light up like a kid in a candy store. The problem is that this often leads to reckless spending, a race against time, and ultimately a cycle of dependency on new funding. Startups become so focused on growth metrics that they forget the fundamentals of running a solid business.

In this frenzy, founders may feel like they're in a race against the clock, desperately trying to prove their worth. But here's the kicker: chasing exponential growth can lead to long-term disaster. Without a solid foundation, what happens when the growth stops? Companies can find themselves with a bloated valuation, high overhead costs, and an unviable business model. It's like building a mansion on a swamp—looks impressive until it all comes crashing down.

Let's face it, expecting every startup to achieve exponential growth is about as realistic as expecting a toddler to perform brain surgery. It's time to recognize that growth takes time, effort, and a solid strategy. Instead of chasing the next shiny metric, founders should focus on building a sustainable business that can weather the storms ahead, rather than crumbling under the weight of unrealistic expectations. Because when the spotlight fades and the confetti settles, what truly matters is whether your startup can stand on its own two feet—exponential growth or not.

So, let's dig deeper into this whole exponential growth expectation thing. It's not just a fancy phrase tossed around in investor meetings; it's a cultural phenomenon in the startup ecosystem. It's as if someone whispered "unicorn" in the ear of every founder, and suddenly everyone believes they need to be the next fairy-tale success story—at all costs.

Take a closer look at the infamous **Zynga**, the gaming company that took social media by storm with its addictive games like FarmVille. In its heyday, Zynga epitomized the growth-at-all-costs mentality. Investors saw skyrocketing numbers and wanted more, more, more. Zynga was pushed to keep churning out new games and features, regardless of whether they made sense or resonated with users. And while they initially celebrated dizzying growth, the cracks began to show. As user engagement dipped and the company failed to adapt, Zynga's valuation plummeted faster than a poorly designed app crashing at launch. Investors learned the hard way that chasing growth without understanding the market led to a major bust.

Now, let's talk about **Blue Apron**—the meal kit delivery service that many thought would change how we cook forever. In the beginning, everything looked rosy. Their user base was expanding, they were plastered all over social media, and investors couldn't throw money at them fast enough. The problem? The growth was built on a fragile model that relied heavily on discounts and promotions to acquire customers. This is like trying to build a house of cards during an earthquake. Once the initial excitement faded, customers didn't stick around. The cost of acquiring new customers was astronomical, and when the company went public, it was like watching a slow-motion train wreck. The stock price plummeted, and the once-celebrated unicorn became a poster child for what happens when growth is pursued without a sustainable plan.

This isn't just about individual companies, though. It speaks to a broader problem in the venture capital world. Investors often push startups to grow at a frenetic pace, expecting them to scale quickly and secure market dominance. But let's be honest—this isn't a fairy tale where every startup gets a happy ending. The pressure to achieve exponential growth can lead to reckless decisions and a lack of focus on long-term sustainability.

Think about **Tesla** for a moment. Here's a company that has undoubtedly achieved incredible growth and has a strong brand. But it's worth noting that Tesla had its fair share of skeptics along the way. Elon Musk's relentless push for innovation and growth has sometimes resulted in chaotic production processes and unmet delivery timelines. When the company fell short of production goals, critics had a field day. And while Tesla has managed to sustain its growth and popularity, the underlying tension between growth and operational efficiency serves as a cautionary tale for many founders. The idea that "you must grow or die" can lead to a death spiral if the growth isn't backed by solid fundamentals.

Let's not forget the lesson from **Oyo Rooms**, which aimed to revolutionize the hospitality industry with a budget-friendly approach. They grew so rapidly that they expanded into international markets without a solid foundation. While they gained massive traction initially, they faced severe backlash regarding service quality and time. It's like watching a magician pull a rabbit out of a hat, only to realize later that the rabbit is just a poorly disguised sock puppet.

In the high-stakes world of startups, sustainability has become the buzzword du jour, the gold star that every founder aims to slap on their business model. But here's the kicker: the illusion of sustainability often involves a lot of smoke and mirrors, and what looks like a thriving ecosystem can be as fragile as a house of cards in a windstorm. Companies might flaunt impressive user numbers, dazzling valuations, and glittering projections, but when you peel back the layers, you might find a pile of mismanaged resources and an unsustainable business model.

Take **Blue Apron**, for example. They burst onto the scene with a ton of fanfare and a subscription meal kit model that made it seem like they had cracked the code to a sustainable business. Initial funding poured in, and their growth was celebrated like a victory parade. But here's the thing: as they scaled, the cracks started to show. The customer acquisition costs soared, and retention rates plummeted. They tried to sustain the illusion of success by continually raising funds and expanding their offerings, but the reality was they were spending far more than they were bringing in. Their impressive initial growth turned into a desperate scramble, and when they finally went public, it became clear that the sustainability they touted was nothing more than a mirage. Their stock plummeted, leaving investors wondering if they'd been duped by a slick marketing campaign.

Then there's **Juicero**, the infamous juice startup that raised $120 million to sell high-tech juicing machines. The illusion of sustainability was so strong that investors bought into the hype. Juicero made a big deal about its technology and the premium product it offered. But guess what? The machines were essentially useless without their proprietary juice packs, which customers could squeeze by hand just as easily. The sustainability of Juicero's model collapsed under the weight of reality when it was revealed that the packs could be opened without the expensive machine. The company floundered and ultimately shut down, proving that their sustainable business model was more like a flimsy balloon—great for show, but unable to withstand the slightest poke.

Even well-established players can fall prey to this illusion. Take **Sears**, which once dominated the retail landscape. For years, they clung to their legacy and tried to sustain their brand by diversifying and offering everything under the sun. They rebranded and pivoted, trying to convince everyone that they were still relevant in a digital world. But beneath the facade of sustainability, they were struggling with outdated business practices and dwindling customer loyalty. Their attempts to reinvent themselves were too little, too late, and eventually, the once-mighty giant fell into bankruptcy. The illusion of sustainability crumbled, leaving a cautionary tale about the dangers of ignoring market shifts while chasing a mirage.

This whole situation is akin to a glamorous party where everyone's dressed to the nines, sipping champagne, and enjoying the festivities, but in the back corner, the host is frantically trying to keep the lights on and prevent the roof from caving in. The facade looks fabulous, but underneath, it's chaos.

The truth is, sustainability requires more than just flashy marketing and buzzwords; it demands a solid foundation, a clear understanding of the market, and a willingness to adapt and innovate. Companies need to shift their focus from chasing ever-inflated valuations to creating genuine value for customers and building resilient business models. Instead of living in a fairy tale world where unicorns roam free, startups should embrace the messy, sometimes painful reality of building something sustainable that can weather the storms of the market.

In a nutshell, the illusion of sustainability can be tempting, but it's a dangerous game. If startups want to thrive in the long run, they need to confront the reality of their business models, be honest about their growth potential, and focus on creating real value for customers. Because let's face it: reality is a harsh mistress, and pretending otherwise can lead to a spectacular downfall.

Early Investors and Their Exit Strategy

The mysterious world of early investors and their ever-elusive exit strategy—a topic that could rival a Shakespearean drama for its intrigue, betrayal, and, of course, tragic outcomes. It's like watching a game of Monopoly where some players are sneaky, waiting for the right moment to cash in on their investments while the rest of the table is oblivious to the fact that they've been meticulously plotting their downfall.

Let's face it: early investors are often the unsung puppeteers in the startup world, orchestrating the grand performance of success while quietly preparing for their exit. They swoop in with a flurry of cash, promising to help founders achieve their lofty dreams, but behind that shiny facade lies a well-thought-out plan to make a graceful exit before the whole thing goes south.

Take **Theranos**, for instance. The biotech startup that promised to revolutionize blood testing caught the attention of investors with its slick pitch and ambitious vision. Early investors were enticed by the prospect of huge returns, jumping in with both feet, seemingly blinded by the potential for fame and fortune. But let's not kid ourselves—these investors weren't in it for the long haul. They were watching the clock, waiting for the right moment to cash out. When the truth about Theranos' technology began to unravel, and the company faced scrutiny and legal troubles, many early investors scrambled for the exits. They had built their castles in the sky, only to find that the foundation was made of quicksand. Their exit strategy was clear: sell before the inevitable collapse, even if it meant leaving others holding the bag.

Then there's **WeWork**, the coworking space giant that was once the darling of the startup scene. Early investors, including some heavy hitters from the venture capital world, poured money into WeWork, dazzled by the vision of a collaborative workspace utopia. But behind the scenes, these investors had a master plan: inflate the valuation, build hype, and then ride the wave to a lucrative exit. When the company attempted to go public, the cracks in its business model were exposed, and the stock tanked faster than a lead balloon. Early investors, however, had already lined their pockets and managed to escape before the chaos unfolded. They'd successfully executed their exit strategy, leaving the founders and late-stage investors to pick up the pieces of a once-promising venture.

Consider the story of **Pets.com** during the dot-com bubble. Early investors eagerly dove into the online pet supply market, convinced that they were riding the wave of the future. They invested millions, and the hype was electric. But once again, the exit strategy became the priority. As the market began to shift, and Pets.com struggled to turn a profit, early investors began to sell off their shares. Before the company crashed spectacularly, they'd already made their exits, cashing in while they could and leaving a trail of chaos in their wake.

This whole dynamic plays out like a game of musical chairs, where the music is the excitement of early funding, and the chairs are the lucrative exit opportunities. As the tempo picks up and the pressure mounts, early investors are primed to make their move, dancing around the chaos while they grab their seats and cash out. Those left standing? Well, good luck dealing with the consequences.

The pressure to maintain high valuations and satisfy early investors often leads to a toxic cycle. Founders feel the heat to keep growing, and early investors are more than happy to stoke the flames. After all, it's not their skin in the game when the house of cards starts to tumble.

Their focus is on the exit, and they'll pull the strings to ensure they're first in line when the time comes.

In the grand scheme of things, this is the cold reality of early investing. It's a calculated game of risk and reward, where the players understand the stakes and strategize their exits long before anyone else even realizes there's a problem. The tragedy is that many founders, swept up in the excitement and optimism of their venture, don't see the storm clouds gathering on the horizon until it's too late.

Ultimately, early investors and their exit strategies illustrate the complex, often ruthless nature of the startup ecosystem. They're the architects of both hype and despair, navigating the landscape with the finesse of seasoned players while founders are left trying to salvage their dreams. It's a lesson in the harsh realities of entrepreneurship: the glitz and glamour of investment can quickly give way to the cold, hard truth of survival in a cutthroat world. If you're a founder, take heed—the game might be rigged, but understanding the rules can help you navigate the treacherous waters ahead.

The Dangers of a Ponzi-Like Structure

The Ponzi-like structure in venture capital—the unsung villain lurking in the shadows of the startup world, ready to sweep you off your feet and then leave you stranded in a financial wasteland. It's like a bad rom-com where the charming lead seems perfect at first, but as the plot unfolds, you realize you're just another pawn in their grand scheme. Spoiler alert: there's no happily ever after when you're caught in a Ponzi scheme, and let's be honest, the narrative rarely ends well for anyone involved.

So, what's the deal with this Ponzi-like structure? Essentially, it's a system built on the premise that new funding rounds keep rolling in, keeping the whole charade afloat. Just like a classic Ponzi scheme, where returns for earlier investors are paid using the investments from new participants, many startups rely on the illusion of endless growth and capital influx to sustain their operations. This leads to a vicious cycle where founders are pressured to keep raising funds, often at the expense of creating a sustainable business model.

Let's take a look at **Uber**, the ride-hailing giant that epitomizes the dangers of this structure. Uber raised billions of dollars in funding, and its early investors were enticed by the promise of exponential growth and dominance in the transportation market. The problem? Uber's business model was built on burning cash to subsidize rides, all while maintaining an unsustainable valuation that depended on the next funding round to keep the lights on. Investors kept pumping money into the company, hoping for that elusive exit when the company finally turned a profit. Meanwhile, the pressure on Uber to continue growing at all costs led to a culture of recklessness, resulting in scandals, lawsuits, and a tarnished reputation. Ultimately, while Uber managed to go public, the company's path has been riddled with challenges, revealing just how fragile that Ponzi-like structure can be.

Now let's throw in a little **Theranos** for good measure. The blood-testing startup had a valuation that soared into the billions, enticing investors with the promise of a revolutionary technology. However, underneath the shiny exterior was a business model built on hype and a desperate need for new funding to keep the illusion alive. Early investors were so focused on their potential returns that they overlooked the fundamental flaws in the technology. As long as the money kept flowing, the company could maintain the façade of success. But when the truth came crashing down, it was like the bubble burst, leaving many investors scrambling for cover and illustrating just how dangerous this Ponzi-like structure can be.

Then there's the infamous **WeWork**, where the magic of a Ponzi-like structure played out with all the drama of a reality TV show. WeWork's valuation skyrocketed based on the belief that it was revolutionizing the office space industry. But the truth? The company was more about style than substance, continually raising funds to cover its massive losses while promising the world to its investors. The moment they tried to go public, the veil was lifted, revealing a shaky business model that relied heavily on continuous funding to stay afloat. Investors quickly realized they were part of a Ponzi-like game, trying to cash out before the whole thing crumbled.

The underlying danger of these Ponzi-like structures is that they create a false sense of security. Founders may feel invincible, riding the wave of hype and funding, while investors blindly chase the next big thing, convinced they'll be the ones who strike gold. But just like a game of Jenga, one wrong move—a missed funding round, a drop in user numbers, or a scandal—can send everything tumbling down. The sense of urgency to raise new funds often leads to poor decision-making, as startups prioritize short-term gains over long-term sustainability. The result? A precarious house of cards that could collapse at any moment, taking everyone down with it.

And let's not forget the impact this has on employees and stakeholders. When a company is operating on a Ponzi-like structure, it's not just the investors who are left holding the bag. Employees can find themselves in a precarious position, their jobs at risk if the company can't secure the next funding round. The promise of stock options and growth can quickly turn into a harsh reality when the whole thing falls apart.

Ultimately, the dangers of a Ponzi-like structure in venture capital serve as a stark reminder of the inherent risks in the startup ecosystem. It's a high-stakes game where the glitz and glamour can quickly fade, revealing the harsh realities of a world built on fragile foundations. As founders, investors, and employees navigate this treacherous landscape, it's crucial to keep a keen eye on the signs of a Ponzi-like structure and remember that in the world of startups, the fairy tale often ends in disaster. So, buckle up and prepare for the ride, because navigating the wild world of venture capital can feel a lot like dancing on a tightrope—one misstep, and you might just find yourself plummeting into the abyss.

Profitability vs. Growth: Why You Can't Have Both

In the dizzying world of startups, there's a mantra that's become almost religious in its fervor: **growth over profitability**. Founders worship at the altar of **exponential expansion**, believing that if they can just scale fast enough, profits will magically follow. Spoiler alert: they won't. We'll dissect the unfortunate truth that chasing growth often means sacrificing profitability on the altar of investor expectations and market hype.

Picture this: you've just launched your startup, and everything is going swimmingly. You've got users flocking to your platform like it's the latest TikTok dance challenge, and venture capitalists are throwing cash at you like confetti at a wedding. You start believing your own hype, thinking that if you just keep the momentum going, your business will eventually become a cash cow. But here's the kicker—**that mindset is as reliable as a blindfolded tightrope walker juggling chainsaws**.

In this chapter, we'll delve into the fundamental conflict at the heart of the modern startup narrative: the relentless pursuit of growth often comes at the expense of financial health. Founders are so focused on attracting users and scaling operations that they neglect the very principles that sustain a business in the long run. Profitability? That's a distant dream, pushed aside like yesterday's leftovers.

We'll also explore case studies that exemplify this troubling trend, like the case of **Uber**, where the company prioritized growth over profitability to the point of absurdity. They burned through billions in subsidies just to gain market share, and while their user base exploded, the reality was that the more they grew, the deeper their losses became. What's the end game here? Spoiler alert: it's not pretty.

In a world where unicorns prance around on clouds of VC funding, the truth is that many of these companies have never turned a profit. They've built empires on sandcastles, relying on the belief that growth alone will validate their existence. But as we'll see, that kind of thinking can lead to catastrophic failures when the reality of sustainability sets in.

So buckle up as we navigate the treacherous waters of profitability versus growth, exposing the harsh truths behind this ubiquitous startup myth. Because in the end, if your business is all about the hustle and you're not keeping an eye on the bottom line, you might just find yourself drowning in a sea of lost investor confidence and empty promises.

The Growth Obsession: Ignoring Financial Health

In the wild, wild west of the startup world, where founders are often lauded as modern-day cowboys riding the tech frontier, there's a dangerous obsession that seems to have taken hold: **growth at all costs**. It's like the startup version of "Get Rich Quick" schemes, where the promise of exponential growth clouds the judgment of even the most rational thinkers. They're so enamored with skyrocketing user numbers and dollar signs that they often forget the basics of sound financial health.

Let's break this down. Imagine a bakery that's selling cupcakes like hotcakes, raking in money hand over fist. The owner is thrilled, investing in a bigger kitchen, hiring staff, and even planning a second location because the first one is bustling. But here's the catch—while the bakery's sales are soaring, the owner is neglecting to track costs, inventory management, or even the profit margins on those delicious treats. Sure, the shop looks busy, but what happens when the costs of ingredients rise, and suddenly the bakery is left with a beautiful shop and a gaping hole in the bank account? Spoiler alert: bankruptcy doesn't care how many cupcakes you sold.

This is the kind of naive enthusiasm that pervades the startup scene, where founders throw caution to the wind in the name of growth. A classic example is **WeWork**. The co-working giant became synonymous with overblown valuations and aggressive expansion. They didn't just rent out office space; they set out to create a global community of entrepreneurs and freelancers, envisioning a utopia of collaboration. But in doing so, they neglected the fundamental question: **Is this sustainable?** WeWork's growth strategy involved leasing vast amounts of prime real estate, furnishing trendy spaces, and rolling out fancy perks, all while racking up massive losses. The company was valued at a whopping $47 billion at one point, but the truth was that they were bleeding cash faster than they could open new locations.

The focus on growth often leads to **blind spots** regarding financial health. Founders start believing their own hype, thinking that as long as they're growing, everything else will fall into place. "Who needs profits when we've got users?" they scoff, pouring money into marketing, talent acquisition, and grandiose plans that often lead to inflated valuations but hollow business fundamentals.

Another striking example is **Snapchat**. The platform famously prioritized growth over profitability in its early days, offering tantalizing features and massive funding rounds that ballooned its valuation. They were so focused on acquiring users that they neglected the basic economics of running a business. The company has consistently struggled to achieve profitability, and despite having millions of active users, the reliance on ad revenue proved to be a double-edged sword. Advertisers want more than just a big audience; they want engaged users who convert into sales. Without that, all those shiny growth figures are little more than glitter sprinkled on a crumbling foundation.

It's crucial to remember that growth isn't inherently bad; it's the **relentless obsession with growth** that can lead startups to ignore the essential building blocks of their business. If you're scaling without a solid financial strategy, you're essentially building a house of cards. One gust of wind—like a market downturn or a shift in consumer behavior—and your beautiful growth story could come crashing down.

At the end of the day, startups must find a balance between growth and financial health. Ignoring the numbers while riding the growth wave is like driving a car with your eyes closed, and the road ahead is full of sharp turns. So, founders, while you're busy counting users, don't forget to check your cash flow because ignoring your financial health is a sure way to derail your growth ambitions faster than you can say, "IPO."

Profitability vs. Growth Metrics

In the high-stakes game of startups, there's a perennial battle waging between two factions: **profitability** and **growth metrics**. Imagine them as rival teams in a never-ending sports match, each with its own fanbase, strategies, and chants. The issue? Profitability is the seasoned veteran with years of experience, while growth metrics is the flashy rookie who just broke the internet with a viral TikTok dance. And what's the result of this face-off? Well, most startups end up sidelined, trying to keep both teams happy while getting absolutely nowhere.

Let's be real: in the startup ecosystem, growth metrics are often celebrated like they're the Holy Grail. Founders plaster their social media with flashy user growth stats, emphasizing how many new users signed up last month, while profitability lurks in the shadows, feeling about as welcome as a rain cloud at a beach party. It's not that growth isn't important; it is. But when startups put growth on a pedestal and profitability gets shunned to the back, they're playing a risky game—like driving a sports car at top speed without checking the fuel gauge.

Take **Uber**, for example. It's a classic case study of the growth obsession. The ride-hailing giant has transformed urban transportation and disrupted traditional taxi services worldwide, all while boasting about its explosive growth metrics. They hit the ground running, offering attractive incentives for both riders and drivers, luring them in with discounts and bonuses. However, the price for that growth has been steep. Uber's path to market dominance was paved with billions in losses. As of 2023, it has only recently begun to show signs of profitability, after years of aggressive expansion that overshadowed its financial health. They were so busy chasing growth metrics that they forgot to ask the million-dollar question: "Are we actually making money here?"

Another cautionary tale is **DoorDash**, the food delivery app that became a household name, especially during the pandemic. The company saw a meteoric rise in users and delivery orders, which propelled its valuation to new heights. Everyone was celebrating the growth; they couldn't deliver food fast enough! But here's the kicker: while DoorDash was riding the wave of user acquisition, they were still grappling with profitability. The high costs of logistics, promotions, and delivery fees turned their shiny growth metrics into a mirage. DoorDash could boast about its expanding user base, but the reality was that they had to deal with a complex web of financial sustainability.

This fixation on growth at the expense of profitability can lead to a **toxic cycle**. Founders raise funding based on impressive growth metrics, believing that more users will magically translate into profit down the line. "If we just get to a million users, we'll figure out the profit later!" they exclaim, pouring cash into marketing and expansion like they're trying to fill a bottomless pit. Yet, without a clear pathway to profitability, that pit only deepens. Eventually, when the funding runs dry and investors start asking tough questions about cash flow, these startups find themselves scrambling to pivot, cut costs, or lay off employees—often too late.

In contrast, startups like **Basecamp** have championed a different philosophy. They focused on building a sustainable business model from the outset, prioritizing profitability over flashy growth metrics. Their steady and sustainable approach has allowed them to thrive without the drama of cash burn and frantic pivots. The lesson? While growth metrics might dazzle investors and make for great headlines, a business that doesn't prioritize profitability is like a beautiful façade hiding a crumbling structure underneath.

Ultimately, the balance between profitability and growth metrics is not just a numbers game; it's about creating a sustainable business that can withstand the inevitable market fluctuations. Founders need to remember that while it's great to celebrate user growth, that applause shouldn't drown out the critical voices asking about profit margins. After all, no one wants to be the startup equivalent of a flashy fireworks show that leaves the audience in awe but disappears without a trace before the morning light. So, it's time for startups to embrace the idea that profitability doesn't kill growth; it fuels it, setting the stage for long-term success rather than a flash-in-the-pan victory.

Case Studies of Profitless Unicorns

In the ever-evolving landscape of startups, many companies have reached unicorn status—valued at over a billion dollars—while simultaneously flaunting the proud distinction of being profitless. These case studies serve as cautionary tales, illustrating the pitfalls of prioritizing growth metrics over profitability. Let's delve into a few high-profile examples of profitless unicorns that are as puzzling as they are eye-opening.

1. Uber

Ah, Uber—the ride-hailing darling that everyone loves to hate. Launched in 2010, it revolutionized the way we think about transportation, connecting passengers with drivers at the tap of a button. Despite its massive growth and market dominance, Uber has never turned a profit since its inception. In fact, as of 2023, Uber reported a staggering cumulative net loss of over $30 billion.

The reason for this phenomenon? Uber's obsession with rapid growth led them to engage in a race to acquire market share, often at unsustainable costs. They offered massive incentives to drivers and discounted rides for customers to lure them into using the platform. While this strategy propelled their user base into the stratosphere, it came at the expense of financial health. Uber has often been forced to raise new funding rounds, relying on investors to keep the lights on. This relentless cycle of growth over profitability reflects a model that many other startups have emulated—only to face similar consequences.

2. WeWork

Let's talk about WeWork, the office-sharing behemoth that aimed to create a global network of shared workspaces. Founded in 2010, WeWork rapidly expanded, raising billions from investors and achieving a staggering valuation of $47 billion at its peak. The company's growth was fueled by an aggressive expansion strategy and a focus on brand-building rather than financial viability.

However, beneath the shiny surface, WeWork was racking up massive losses, largely due to its business model, which involved long-term leases and short-term rental agreements. This imbalance meant that even with high occupancy rates, the company struggled to turn a profit. By 2019, as scrutiny intensified around its financial practices and the eccentric behavior of its founder Adam Neumann, WeWork's valuation plummeted, and it eventually filed for an IPO, revealing the harsh reality of its profitless existence. The story of WeWork is a textbook example of a startup that prioritized growth and branding over sustainability, leading to a spectacular crash and burn.

3. DoorDash

Next up is DoorDash, a food delivery service that exploded onto the scene, especially during the COVID-19 pandemic when takeout became the norm. In 2020, DoorDash experienced astronomical growth, capturing significant market share and drawing attention from hungry investors. However, while the user numbers soared, profitability remained elusive.

DoorDash's business model relied heavily on promotions and discounts to attract users, which, while effective in the short term, eroded profit margins. The company has faced criticisms for the high delivery fees imposed on customers and low compensation for drivers, which led to ongoing debates about sustainability. Although DoorDash eventually went public in late 2020, it still struggles with profitability, highlighting the precarious balance between rapid growth and financial health.

4. Lyft

Uber's rival Lyft has also found itself in a similar predicament. Established in 2012, Lyft quickly carved out a niche in the ride-sharing market, focusing on a friendly and community-driven image. Despite its popularity and growing user base, Lyft has consistently reported losses, with billions in red ink since its founding.

Much like Uber, Lyft adopted a growth-at-all-costs strategy, offering discounts and incentives to compete with its larger rival. While it managed to attract users and expand into new markets, the strategy led to financial instability. In 2022, Lyft reported an annual loss of over $1 billion, prompting discussions about whether the company could pivot towards profitability in an industry characterized by fierce competition and fluctuating demand.

5. Peloton

Let's not forget Peloton, the fitness equipment company that transformed home workouts with its interactive exercise bikes and streaming classes. Founded in 2012, Peloton enjoyed explosive growth, especially during the pandemic, as people turned to home fitness solutions. Valued at $50 billion at its peak, Peloton became a symbol of the fitness revolution.

However, the company struggled to maintain that momentum post-pandemic. Peloton's model relied heavily on subscriptions and a high upfront cost for its equipment, leading to questions about sustainability. With rising costs and slowing sales, Peloton reported significant losses in 2021, prompting layoffs and restructuring. This scenario underscores how the lure of rapid growth can create a false sense of security, masking underlying financial instability.

In conclusion, these case studies of profitless unicorns illustrate the dangers of prioritizing growth over profitability. While it's easy to get swept up in the excitement of soaring user numbers and investor hype, the sobering reality is that many of these companies have built their empires on shaky foundations. As they navigate the murky waters of the startup ecosystem, it becomes clear that chasing unicorn status without a sustainable path to profitability can lead to a spectacular fall from grace. Founders must learn from these cautionary tales, recognizing that in the world of startups, it's not just about how fast you grow; it's also about how well you manage the cash flow to ensure longevity.

The Pressure to Pivot to Profitability

In the high-stakes world of startups, the relentless pursuit of growth often leads companies into a vicious cycle where profitability becomes a mere afterthought. However, as the startup landscape evolves and investor expectations shift, the pressure to pivot to profitability becomes a reality that many unicorns must confront—often too late. Let's explore this phenomenon, why it's essential, and how companies can (or often fail to) navigate the treacherous waters of transitioning from growth-at-all-costs to a sustainable business model.

The moment that investors begin to whisper the dreaded "P" word—profitability—things can get dicey. Suddenly, the dream of scaling at lightning speed morphs into a frantic scramble to figure out how to keep the lights on while meeting lofty expectations. This shift often feels like trying to turn a massive ship on a dime; it's clumsy, and by the time you're pointed in the right direction, you may already have lost your course—or worse, capsized.

As startups scale, they often build expansive teams, invest in flashy marketing campaigns, and engage in costly customer acquisition strategies. Yet, when the financial reports begin to reveal an unsustainable burn rate, investors start to get antsy. Their once boundless enthusiasm for growth can quickly turn into an anxiety-fueled quest for profit. It's almost like watching a soap opera unfold: one minute, you're on cloud nine, celebrating record user growth, and the next, you're grappling with the reality of mounting losses and investors breathing down your neck.

For many companies, this pressure to pivot to profitability arrives unexpectedly. A great example is Snapchat. The social media platform initially captured the hearts of millions with its disappearing messages and innovative features. However, as Snap's stock price plummeted after its IPO, the pressure to pivot to profitability intensified. The company was forced to cut costs, reduce its workforce, and rethink its monetization strategy. All of a sudden, Snapchat had to ditch its carefree, youthful image and start looking more like a responsible adult, scrutinizing every expense and revenue stream in an effort to appease its investors.

Transitioning to profitability often requires a dramatic shift in company culture and strategy. This can be akin to a teenager suddenly being told to take on adult responsibilities: it's awkward, messy, and filled with a lot of eye-rolling. Companies frequently need to reassess their business models. For instance, Blue Apron, the meal kit delivery service, experienced significant growth early on but faced intense scrutiny as it struggled to turn a profit. As customer acquisition costs ballooned and competition surged, Blue Apron was forced to reconsider its pricing strategy, shift to a more subscription-focused model, and even explore partnerships with other grocery retailers to stabilize revenue streams.

When the pressure mounts, many startups go into panic mode, leading to drastic measures. Think about WeWork. They expanded at breakneck speed, scooping up real estate and brand partnerships left and right. But when the narrative shifted from "unicorn" to "messy breakup," WeWork found itself in a tailspin, needing to cut back on its extravagant spending and focus on its core business—something they had lost sight of amid their growth obsession. They learned the hard way that you can't just charm your way to profitability; you need a sound strategy that doesn't resemble a house of cards.

The pressure to pivot can be brutal, with many startups fumbling in the dark, trying to find their footing. And while some companies manage to adapt, others become tragic cautionary tales. Take **Zynga**, for example. The company rode high on the waves of social gaming but struggled to pivot to sustainable profitability. It faced fierce competition and changing user preferences, which led to a sharp decline in user engagement and revenue. Zynga's frantic attempts to salvage profitability—like slashing costs and churning out sequels—didn't prevent its stock from tanking.

Navigating the treacherous waters between growth and profitability can feel like trying to cross a tightrope while juggling flaming torches—exciting, yet perilously risky. The pressure to pivot to profitability is an intense experience that forces startups to reassess their strategies, often revealing whether they can thrive in a competitive landscape or simply flounder.

Consider **Uber**, the poster child for the growth-at-all-costs mentality. For years, the ride-hailing giant poured money into market expansion, driver incentives, and customer promotions, all while proudly flaunting its skyrocketing user numbers. However, despite achieving dizzying heights, the profitability question loomed ominously over them. Uber's relentless quest for dominance led to a burn rate that made investors sweat. With its public offering approaching, the company faced mounting pressure to prove it could actually turn a profit. In response, Uber implemented various measures, including cost-cutting initiatives and increasing fares, but the transition was anything but seamless. They had to balance their ambitions with the harsh reality that, at some point, investors would want to see returns, not just a growing number of app downloads. It was like watching a magician who finally has to reveal how all the tricks are done.

Then there's **Peloton**, which rode the wave of fitness enthusiasm during the pandemic. Initially, the company enjoyed massive growth, attracting millions of subscribers and selling high-end exercise bikes at an impressive clip. But as the world opened back up, the company's growth trajectory stalled, and it found itself grappling with the consequences of its expansion. As consumer interest waned, Peloton had to make the painful decision to lay off staff and reassess its pricing strategies. The company learned that while it was fun to ride the wave of initial success, when the tide receded, it had to scramble to demonstrate profitability. The pressure to pivot became a frantic scramble, turning fitness enthusiasts into anxious investors.

Let's also take a look at **Theranos**, a cautionary tale of how the pressure to succeed can lead to disastrous consequences. The company, once hailed as a revolutionary health tech startup, raised hundreds of millions in funding based on its promise to deliver blood testing technology that required only a single drop of blood. As expectations soared, the pressure to prove its profitability intensified. In a desperate bid to maintain its illusion of success, Theranos resorted to unethical practices, ultimately leading to its spectacular collapse. The founders were so engrossed in creating a narrative of growth and innovation that they lost sight of the fundamental need for transparency and accountability, leaving them and their investors in a pile of rubble.

Another noteworthy example is **WeWork**, which tried to make workspaces as trendy as avocado toast. They expanded rapidly, acquiring prime real estate and branding themselves as a lifestyle choice for professionals. However, the company's flashy growth came at a steep price, and when it was time for their IPO, the reality set in. WeWork's valuation plummeted from $47 billion to a mere $8 billion almost overnight as investors demanded to know how the company planned to turn a profit amidst its lavish spending. It became painfully clear that the growth they had so eagerly pursued was masking significant financial instability. WeWork's journey is a perfect illustration of how the pursuit of growth without a sustainable plan can lead to a catastrophic fall from grace.

And we can't forget about **Blue Apron**, which initially thrived by selling meal kits to a health-conscious audience. However, as competitors entered the market, Blue Apron struggled to maintain its growth and started offering deep discounts to attract customers. The pressure to pivot toward profitability forced Blue Apron to rethink its model, but by then, they had already set a precedent of relying on discounts, leading to a fragile customer base. The company's journey serves as a testament to the perils of prioritizing short-term growth strategies over sustainable business practices.

Even **DoorDash** faced its fair share of challenges. After enjoying massive growth during the pandemic, it found itself in the hot seat post-IPO, where it was expected to show that it could continue to thrive. The company began to focus on strategies to pivot to profitability, like diversifying its services and implementing delivery fees. However, this led to backlash from users who had gotten used to the pre-IPO era of low fees and discounts. DoorDash had to walk a tightrope, balancing the need to maintain user loyalty while also appeasing investors with promises of profitability.

Ultimately, the path to profitability isn't just about cutting costs or changing the business model. It's about embracing a mindset that prioritizes sustainable growth rather than an insatiable hunger for market share. Startups need to recognize that profitability isn't the enemy of growth; it's the foundation upon which true success is built.

So, while the allure of rapid scaling and explosive growth can be intoxicating, it's crucial to keep one eye on the bottom line. As companies navigate the stormy seas of investor expectations and market realities, the ability to pivot towards profitability—without losing sight of their core mission—will determine who survives the treacherous journey in the startup ecosystem.

Long-Term Implications of Growth-Only Focus

Focusing solely on growth, while an exhilarating ride in the short term, often leads to long-term implications that can be as disastrous as a plane crash in slow motion. Let's dig into the grim consequences of this growth-only mentality and how it can haunt companies for years, leaving them scrambling to put out fires while pretending everything is fine.

When companies prioritize growth over all else, they often make decisions that are reckless, like buying a sports car on credit and then wondering how to pay for gas. For example, many startups start pouring resources into aggressive marketing strategies without truly understanding their target audience or the market dynamics. This can lead to a customer base that is both expensive to acquire and difficult to retain, resulting in what's known as high churn rates. In simple terms, it's like inviting a ton of guests to a party but having them leave early because the vibe is off. Imagine spending a fortune on appetizers only to realize nobody likes the hors d'oeuvres—you're left with an awkward silence and a pile of uneaten food.

Let's consider **Quibi**, the short-lived streaming service that promised to revolutionize on-the-go content consumption. They raised nearly $2 billion in funding, fueled by a relentless growth mindset that ignored crucial market signals. Their massive ad spend and ambitious marketing blitz attracted attention, but the service failed to resonate with viewers. Quibi's growth-only strategy blinded them to the reality that they needed to understand consumer preferences and adapt their offering. When the dust settled, Quibi folded in less than a year, serving as a grim reminder that all the growth in the world means nothing if you can't deliver a product people actually want.

Additionally, when companies obsess over growth metrics, they often sacrifice quality. Think of it this way: if a restaurant focused only on serving as many customers as possible without ensuring the quality of their food, they might attract a crowd at first, but eventually, diners would get turned off by the subpar meals. Take **Yahoo** as an example; once a tech giant, they pursued rapid growth by acquiring numerous companies, often without proper integration or strategy. In the end, this growth-at-all-costs approach led to a fragmented platform that couldn't compete with more focused competitors like Google, resulting in a swift decline and eventual acquisition by Verizon at a fraction of its former glory.

This focus on growth also has a chilling effect on company culture. When the bottom line takes precedence over employee satisfaction, it breeds disillusionment among the workforce. Imagine a workplace where employees are pushed to their limits, working long hours with no regard for their well-being, just to chase the elusive growth target. This leads to burnout, high turnover rates, and a toxic work environment. Companies like **Amazon** have faced criticism for their demanding work conditions, leading to questions about the sustainability of their growth model. While they have grown into one of the largest companies in the world, reports of employee dissatisfaction reveal that growth comes at a steep price. When employees feel undervalued, the quality of work diminishes, and creativity stalls, ultimately stunting the company's long-term potential.

Another significant implication is the inability to pivot when the market demands it. Startups that prioritize growth often become so entrenched in their model that they fail to adapt when necessary. Look at **MySpace**, which was once the leading social media platform, but as it chased growth through user acquisition, it ignored the evolving landscape of social media and failed to innovate. By the time they attempted to pivot, it was too late, and users had flocked to Facebook, leaving MySpace to become a mere relic of the past. It serves as a stark reminder that a fixation on growth can lead to stagnation, rendering companies unable to respond to market changes.

Moreover, a growth-only approach often leads to unsustainable financial practices. Startups may find themselves in a vicious cycle of taking on more debt to fund their expansion, only to face the reality of mounting financial obligations when the growth slows. This is akin to living in a lavish mansion on a tight budget—sure, it looks great, but when the bills come in, you're left scrambling for cash. When these companies can no longer meet investor expectations, they may resort to desperate measures, like layoffs or selling assets, which can further damage their reputation and hinder future growth opportunities.

The long-term implications of a growth-only focus often create a snowball effect of failures and missed opportunities. Companies that neglect profitability, quality, and employee well-being will eventually find themselves in a precarious position. To survive in the startup ecosystem, a balanced approach that prioritizes sustainable growth, innovation, and financial health is crucial. Startups must learn from the mistakes of others and remember that while chasing growth is exhilarating, it should never come at the expense of the foundations that make a company truly successful.

In the end, navigating the startup world requires a careful balance between growth and sustainability. By embracing a holistic approach, companies can build a solid foundation that will withstand the test of time, turning potential pitfalls into stepping stones for long-term success. So, if you're a founder, take a moment to reflect: is your growth strategy built on solid ground, or is it just a house of cards waiting to tumble down?

The Cult of the Founder

In the startup world, there's a kind of reverence surrounding founders that borders on the religious. We'll unravel the mythos that has grown around these entrepreneurial demigods and examine the consequences of this idolization.

Founders are often celebrated as visionaries, rock stars, and even saviors of the modern economy. The media hangs on their every word, investors shower them with cash, and employees are led to believe they're part of a revolutionary movement. But let's get real for a moment: this cult-like devotion can lead to a dangerous disconnect between the founder's vision and the actual sustainability of their companies. It's a love fest that can turn into a horror show faster than you can say "unicorn."

The narrative is usually the same—founders are portrayed as fearless leaders who've overcome insurmountable odds to create their groundbreaking products. This creates a halo effect, where their decisions are rarely questioned, no matter how questionable they might be. Sure, they may have had a brilliant idea, but the reality is that many of these founders lack the experience or business acumen to turn their dreams into sustainable realities. Instead, they end up being worshiped like rock stars, while their companies spiral into chaos.

This chapter will explore the psychology behind this cult of personality, from the way stories are crafted to elevate founders into legends to the consequences of overlooking fundamental business practices in favor of chasing the allure of a charismatic leader. We'll dive into how the glorification of founders can blind investors and employees alike to red flags, leading to poor decision-making and, ultimately, failure.

So buckle up, because we're about to take a hard look at the cult of the founder and how it shapes the landscape of startups, often for the worse.

The Founder's Role: Driving the Hype

In the startup universe, founders are not just the people who come up with the big idea; they are the charismatic leaders who drive the hype train, often at breakneck speed. These founders wield their personal brands like weapons, crafting narratives that seduce investors, customers, and employees alike. They are the star players on this stage, and everyone else is just part of the supporting cast, clapping along to the beat of their vision.

Take Elon Musk, for instance. When he launched SpaceX, he didn't just sell rockets; he sold a dream—colonizing Mars, making humanity a multiplanetary species. Every tweet, every public appearance is steeped in hype that rallies people around his vision, leading them to believe they are part of something monumental. Investors line up like fans outside a concert venue, eager to get a piece of the action because who wouldn't want to ride the coattails of a supposed genius? But let's not forget the flip side: sometimes this level of hype can be a double-edged sword. When things don't go as planned, the fallout can be catastrophic, like a rock star crashing and burning on stage.

Founders craft narratives that transform simple products into life-changing innovations. Take the founders of Airbnb, for example. They didn't just create a platform for booking homes; they spun a tale of community, belonging, and adventure that turned a bunch of random living rooms into "Airbnbs" worldwide. Their ability to weave a compelling narrative turned their venture into a cultural phenomenon, making investors drool and customers flock to their app. But let's not kid ourselves—this level of storytelling can lead to unrealistic expectations. When a company is built more on hype than on sound business practices, you might as well be waiting for a unicorn to prance through your office.

The problem arises when founders get so wrapped up in their own hype that they lose sight of what really matters: the business. They may think they're revolutionizing an industry, but often they're just rehashing existing ideas with a fresh coat of paint and a catchy slogan. Look at the rise of "disruptive" companies—how many times have we heard that term thrown around like confetti at a wedding? It's become so commonplace that it's almost lost its meaning. Just because you're slapping the word "disruptive" on your business plan doesn't mean you're actually doing anything new or meaningful.

Now, let's not forget the consequences of this hyper-focus on the founder's narrative. When investors and employees buy into the hype without questioning the fundamentals, they're essentially setting themselves up for failure. The cult of the founder often leads to a lack of accountability. Mistakes are brushed under the rug because who would dare challenge the brilliant visionary? This creates an environment where founders can make questionable decisions with little to no pushback, leading their companies down a treacherous path.

In a landscape filled with inflated valuations and unrealistic expectations, it's crucial to recognize that founders, while often brilliant and charismatic, are still human. They can't always see beyond their own hype. If everyone's too busy drinking the Kool-Aid, no one's watching for the warning signs. Just look at companies like Theranos, where Elizabeth Holmes became the poster child for the founder cult, and we all know how that story ended. The obsession with her vision overshadowed the numerous red flags, ultimately leading to a catastrophic collapse.

So while it's easy to be swept up in the founder hype, it's important to maintain a level of skepticism. The next time a founder waltzes in with a grand vision, remember that behind the hype lies the actual business, and that's where the real work happens.

Let's dive deeper into the fascinating—and often chaotic—world of the founder cult, where charisma, grand visions, and hype can sometimes overshadow reality, leading to both meteoric rises and spectacular falls.

Consider **Elizabeth Holmes** of **Theranos** fame. Here was a founder whose narrative was so compelling that it captivated Silicon Valley, high-profile investors, and even former presidents. She spun a tale about revolutionizing blood testing—turning dozens of tests into a single drop of blood. It sounded like magic, and investors lined up, eager to buy into the dream. But let's face it; when the technology was scrutinized, it turned out to be about as reliable as a cheap watch from a gas station. The whole operation relied on the charisma and vision of Holmes, which created an environment where critical voices were drowned out. Her narrative had built such an impenetrable fortress of hype that many ignored the glaring issues lurking just beyond the walls. By the time the truth surfaced, the fallout was catastrophic—not just for Holmes but for everyone who had bought into the myth.

Then there's **Adam Neumann** from **WeWork**. Neumann didn't just sell shared office space; he sold a lifestyle, branding WeWork as a community for the "creative class." He was a master at weaving narratives that made the company feel like more than just a place to work; it was a movement! Investors were entranced, and Neumann was lauded as a visionary—until the company went public and the financials revealed that it was all a smoke-and-mirrors show. The financials showed massive losses, and the dream started to crumble. The cult of the founder created an atmosphere where the focus was on Neumann's charisma and his grand vision rather than on sustainable business practices. When the hype train derailed, it wasn't just Neumann who suffered; thousands of employees and investors were left picking up the pieces.

On a slightly less dramatic note, let's talk about **Elon Musk** again. While he's undoubtedly a genius, his unfiltered tweets and over-the-top promises about Tesla can sometimes feel like a tech version of a carnival barker, enticing you into a show that may not live up to the hype. Musk has claimed that Tesla would reach full self-driving capabilities "next year" for several years running. As he continues to set ambitious timelines, investors and fans hang on his every word, often overlooking the hurdles Tesla faces in technology, regulation, and safety. The cult of Musk creates a blind faith in his vision, leading to an environment where timelines and deliverables become more about maintaining the hype than about actual product viability. When the self-driving car isn't ready, and the promised timelines come and go, it raises questions about whether the company is being run by a visionary or a very talented showman.

Let's also examine **Reed Hastings** and **Netflix**. Hastings' vision of streaming content and on-demand viewing was revolutionary. However, as Netflix rapidly scaled and invested heavily in original content, it created a narrative of endless growth. The focus on "growth at all costs" led to massive expenditures, which in turn pushed the company into a massive debt spiral. Hastings' personal brand and the cult-like following of Netflix had investors eager to throw money at the company, even as its profit margins dwindled. But when the streaming wars intensified, and competitors like Disney+ and HBO Max entered the ring, Netflix's growth slowed, exposing the unsustainable nature of its hype-driven model. Suddenly, the company that everyone thought was invincible had to pivot and focus on profitability—something they had been sidelining in favor of growth metrics.

And let's not forget the disastrous impact of the pandemic on **WeWork**. Their narrative was so compelling that they were on track to become a unicorn, but when remote work became the norm, the whole idea of shared office space felt less appealing. The cult of Neumann had convinced everyone that remote work was a temporary inconvenience, and investors overlooked the fundamental shifts in workplace dynamics. This blind faith in the founder's narrative left them exposed when the market shifted overnight.

These examples illustrate the fundamental problem with the cult of the founder: when the vision becomes the priority over the actual mechanics of running a sustainable business, it sets everyone up for a rude awakening. When the hype fades, and the reality hits, the consequences can be devastating.

Now, let's zoom out and think about the culture this creates. When everyone is so enamored with the founder, the organization may become insular, unwilling to challenge the status quo. This could lead to a situation where critical feedback is stifled, and employees are discouraged from voicing concerns. The higher-ups may become so blinded by their belief in the founder's vision that they ignore basic business principles, leading to a kind of corporate groupthink that can spiral out of control.

The stories of founders like Holmes, Neumann, and Hastings should serve as cautionary tales. While founders can indeed drive innovation and inspire those around them, it's crucial to maintain a sense of reality. The next time you hear a founder spinning a grand narrative, remember: it's essential to look beyond the hype and examine what's actually going on beneath the surface. Only by doing so can you navigate the turbulent waters of the startup world without getting swept away by the cult of the founder.

Crafting Founder Stories for Investment

Crafting compelling founder stories is like a high-stakes game of narrative poker—you need to show just enough of your hand to get investors to raise the stakes, but not so much that they see the bluffs. It's an art form, really, where emotion, vision, and a sprinkle of dramatic flair can turn an average founder into the next tech messiah. So, how do you master the art of storytelling without descending into a pit of deceit?

Let's look at **Howard Schultz** of **Starbucks**. When Schultz stepped onto the scene, he didn't just sell coffee; he sold a lifestyle and an experience. He painted a picture of a "third place" between home and work, where customers could gather and connect. The story of Schultz's upbringing in a poor neighborhood, along with his vision of transforming coffee into a communal experience, gave investors something to latch onto beyond financial metrics. It was more than just beans and brews; it was a movement! Investors couldn't resist backing someone who was so passionate about creating a unique experience.

Then there's the ever-quotable **Gary Vaynerchuk**. With his larger-than-life personality, Gary turned his personal brand into a multi-million dollar empire. His story isn't just about building a business; it's about hustle, grit, and the relentless pursuit of passion. By sharing his immigrant roots, his early days selling wine, and his no-nonsense approach to business, he cultivates an aura of authenticity that draws in not just customers but investors who want to be part of the ride. Investors want to believe they're investing in a person, not just a product, and Gary's story sells that belief.

Sara Blakely, the founder of **Spanx**, offers another example of how a personal narrative can enhance investment appeal. Blakely's journey from selling fax machines to launching a billion-dollar shapewear empire is both relatable and inspirational. She often shares the struggles she faced as a female entrepreneur in a male-dominated industry and how she bootstrapped her way to success with $5,000. This narrative resonates with investors who appreciate the tenacity and resourcefulness that come with overcoming obstacles. By positioning herself as a pioneer in her field, Blakely attracts investors who want to support a brand that embodies resilience and innovation.

But it's not all sunshine and rainbows. There's a fine line between crafting a compelling story and creating a narrative that feels like smoke and mirrors. Take the example of **Elizabeth Holmes** from **Theranos** again. Her origin story was expertly crafted—she claimed to be on a mission to democratize healthcare, to make blood testing accessible to everyone. Investors were seduced by the tale, forgetting to look closely at the technology behind the curtain. When the hype unraveled, it became a stark reminder that a good story can only carry you so far; eventually, the product must back it up.

Let's also talk about the infamous **Reed Hastings** and Netflix. Initially, the story was one of innovation: disrupting how we consume media. But as Netflix grew, the narrative shifted, with Hastings spinning tales of endless content and an insatiable appetite for subscriber growth. The more the story shifted toward growth metrics, the more the actual sustainability of the business became clouded. Investors were drawn to the vision of a media giant but may have overlooked the mounting debts and unsustainable practices. Hastings' ability to craft a compelling narrative was ultimately overshadowed by the company's struggle to pivot to profitability.

When crafting these stories, it's crucial to balance ambition with authenticity. It's tempting to embellish the narrative to make it sound more enticing, but if investors sense they've been sold a fairy tale rather than a realistic vision, they're likely to back away. The best founder stories connect on a human level; they're relatable and grounded in truth. So, whether you're sharing the struggles you faced in launching your startup or the vision that keeps you awake at night, keep it real.

The takeaway here? When constructing a narrative for investment, think of it like cooking a gourmet meal. You need the right ingredients—a dash of struggle, a pinch of vision, and a healthy dose of authenticity. When you serve it up, make sure it looks appetizing and smells delicious, but above all, ensure that it's a dish that can withstand scrutiny. After all, no one wants to invest in a story that's all sizzle and no steak.

The Idolization of Founders

The idolization of founders is a phenomenon that transforms ordinary entrepreneurs into rock stars, complete with fan clubs and merchandise. You've seen it: founders who were once just regular folks pitching ideas in coffee shops suddenly find themselves being compared to legends like Steve Jobs or Elon Musk. This blind adoration often leads to an unrealistic expectation of infallibility, and suddenly, every word that slips from their lips is gospel.

Take **Elon Musk**, for instance. Love him or hate him, Musk has managed to become the face of innovation. He doesn't just run companies; he's a full-blown celebrity. The cult of personality surrounding him has led fans to overlook the numerous times his ventures seemed to be teetering on the edge of disaster—like when Tesla was on the brink of bankruptcy or when he tweeted about taking Tesla private at $420 a share, causing quite the commotion. Fans were quick to defend him, insisting he was a genius navigating uncharted waters, while skeptics pointed to his erratic behavior as a sign of instability. But no matter the opinion, his influence is undeniable, and that's what idolization does—it elevates the founder to a status where they can do no wrong, even in the face of glaring failures.

Then there's **Travis Kalanick**, the co-founder of **Uber**. At the height of Uber's meteoric rise, Kalanick was revered as the maverick who was changing the transportation industry. His aggressive tactics and disregard for regulatory hurdles painted him as a rebellious hero. However, when the company faced allegations of a toxic workplace culture and numerous scandals, the facade began to crumble. Despite his past idolization, many started to question whether Kalanick's unchecked ambition was worth the price. The ultimate irony? The very qualities that made him a darling in the startup world also contributed to his downfall, leading to his ouster from the company. It's a classic case of the hero's journey gone wrong, showing that idolization can quickly turn to vilification when the narrative shifts.

But it's not just the rock stars of Silicon Valley who experience this phenomenon. Consider **Elizabeth Holmes**, the founder of **Theranos**. In her early days, she was the darling of the tech world, lauded for her vision of revolutionizing blood testing. Investors and media alike fell under her spell, fawning over her ambitions and seemingly flawless persona. As her story unraveled, however, the cult of the founder began to resemble a tragic comedy—she went from being an idol to a cautionary tale. People often forget that behind the bright-eyed dreams and polished pitches lies a very real person who can make devastating mistakes. The idolization led many to overlook critical flaws in her business model, and when the truth came out, it was nothing short of disastrous.

The core issue here is that the founder myth often overshadows the importance of a strong team, sound business practices, and a realistic approach to growth. Founders are humans, not deities. Yet, in the startup ecosystem, we often forget this vital truth. Investors and employees alike can fall into the trap of projecting their hopes and dreams onto these founders, leading to a form of dependency that can stifle critical thinking and accountability.

Consider the story of **Evan Spiegel** and **Snapchat**. Spiegel's youth and confidence created a magnetic appeal, and for a time, he was treated like a visionary. His concept of disappearing messages resonated with the millennial crowd, and investors threw money at him as if he were the next Zuckerberg. However, when Snapchat struggled to adapt to competition from Instagram and failed to turn a profit for years, the glow of idolization dimmed. Suddenly, investors were asking hard questions instead of blindly fawning over his every move. The backlash from the once-adoring public was swift, and Spiegel's image transformed from a genius to someone whose brilliance was called into question.

Idolization can create a culture of fear and silence among employees. When a founder becomes untouchable, team members may hesitate to speak up about issues or concerns, fearing they'll upset the golden goose. This atmosphere breeds toxicity and can lead to disastrous outcomes, as evidenced by numerous tech startups that implode under the weight of their founder's unchecked power. The infamous example of **WeWork** and its co-founder **Adam Neumann** highlights this issue perfectly. Neumann's extravagant lifestyle and erratic decision-making were often overlooked because he was viewed as a visionary. It wasn't until the disastrous IPO attempt and subsequent financial collapse that the reality set in: the cult of Neumann had blinded many to the fundamental flaws in his leadership and strategy.

Ultimately, the idolization of founders serves as a double-edged sword. It can propel companies to unimaginable heights, as investors and employees rally around a charismatic leader. But it can also create an environment ripe for disaster when accountability takes a backseat to the cult of personality. As we navigate this wild world of startups, it's essential to remember that while founders may lead the charge, they are not infallible gods. They need checks and balances, grounded perspectives, and, most importantly, a team that can voice dissent without fear of repercussions. If not, we risk creating more cautionary tales than success stories.

When the Cult of the Founder Fails

When the cult of the founder fails, it's like watching a superhero fall from grace—complete with dramatic music and a slow-motion plunge. We've seen it too many times in the startup world. It's the moment when the once-revered leader is unmasked, revealing the human flaws and fallacies hidden beneath the glossy PR veneer. What's fascinating (and often cringeworthy) is how quickly the narrative shifts from idolization to ostracism.

Let's take a closer look at the case of **Elizabeth Holmes**, the founder of **Theranos**. For a while, she was hailed as the "next Steve Jobs," complete with turtlenecks and grand visions of transforming healthcare. Investors were all in, lured by her charisma and the promise of a revolutionary blood-testing technology that could perform dozens of tests from a single drop of blood. It was as if she had waved a magic wand and transformed herself into a Silicon Valley sorceress. But when the truth came to light—that the technology was a sham and patients were misled—suddenly, the idolization turned into a full-blown witch hunt. She went from being celebrated as a visionary to being vilified as a fraud. Investors lost millions, and the once-sparkling narrative about a healthcare revolution became a cautionary tale about the dangers of blind faith in charismatic leaders.

Another example is **Travis Kalanick** from **Uber**. Initially, he was seen as the rebellious entrepreneur who was reshaping urban transportation. His relentless push for growth and his willingness to ignore regulations made him a darling of the startup ecosystem. But as scandals piled up—allegations of a toxic work culture, legal battles, and his infamous *"screw you, I'm the boss"* attitude—people began to question if he was the visionary everyone thought he was or just a reckless cowboy with a high-risk strategy. His ultimate ouster was a brutal wake-up call, showing how the idolization of founders can backfire spectacularly when the hype isn't backed by ethical leadership or sound business practices.

We also can't forget about **Adam Neumann**, the co-founder of **WeWork**. At the height of the company's growth, he was celebrated as a revolutionary leader who was going to change the way people work. Investors poured money into the company, believing Neumann's vision for communal workspace was the future. But when WeWork's IPO plans unraveled and his extravagant lifestyle (think private jets, parties, and questionable business practices) came under scrutiny, the narrative flipped. He went from being a visionary to a punchline, and the cult of Neumann crumbled. The aftermath was a disaster not just for Neumann but for thousands of employees and investors who believed in the hype.

Even outside the tech bubble, we see similar patterns. Consider **Howard Schultz** of **Starbucks**. He was revered for transforming a small coffee chain into a global phenomenon. However, his attempts to return to the company amid labor disputes and changing consumer habits led to criticisms about his relevance and adaptability. The idolization that once propelled his decisions became a double-edged sword, as stakeholders began to question if his old-school tactics could still apply in a new age of consumer activism and ethical business practices.

When the cult of the founder fails, it's not just about the individual's downfall; it often triggers a domino effect that impacts the entire company and its stakeholders. Employees who once believed in the founder's vision may find themselves disillusioned, investors face significant losses, and customers can lose trust in the brand. The company that once seemed destined for greatness may suddenly find itself in a tailspin, struggling to recover from the fallout.

In many cases, the failure of the cult of the founder reveals a deeper issue within the startup ecosystem—an unhealthy dependency on a single individual. This can stifle innovation and critical thinking, as everyone waits for the founder's next move instead of contributing their ideas. As we've seen time and again, when the hype fades and the harsh light of reality shines through, the cracks in the foundation become all too apparent.

So, the next time you find yourself swept up in the cult of a founder, take a moment to remember: they're human, just like the rest of us. And while they may have charisma and vision, it's essential to keep a level head and demand accountability. Because when the idol falls, the impact is often more profound than the initial rise to glory.

Lessons Learned from Founder Failures

The drama of founder failures isn't just a cautionary tale; it's a masterclass in what *not* to do in the startup world. Each epic fall from grace is riddled with lessons, and if we're smart enough to pay attention, we can glean some wisdom from these spectacular train wrecks.

First and foremost, **diversifying leadership** is crucial. Relying too heavily on a single individual for vision and direction is like building a house on sand—eventually, it's going to crumble. The **WeWork** saga exemplifies this perfectly. When Adam Neumann was at the helm, the company's strategy, culture, and decision-making were all centered around him. Once the cracks started to show, there was no backup plan or leadership structure to stabilize the ship. By cultivating a strong, diverse leadership team, companies can safeguard against the pitfalls of founder-centric decision-making.

Next, we should never underestimate the power of **transparency and accountability**. The aura of mystery surrounding a founder can often lead to unchecked power and a lack of oversight. Look at **Theranos** and Elizabeth Holmes; the opacity of their operations allowed problems to fester unchecked. If founders were required to operate with transparency—sharing progress, setbacks, and failures—investors and employees would be better equipped to assess the health of the company realistically. Instead of a "trust me" mentality, fostering an environment of openness encourages healthy skepticism, which can prevent catastrophic misjudgments.

Another critical lesson is to **embrace a growth mindset**, which includes the ability to pivot and adapt when things go south. Founders often become enamored with their initial vision, causing them to cling to outdated strategies even when the market is shifting. Remember the downfall of **Blockbuster**? They were so focused on their rental model that they ignored the rise of digital streaming. Contrast that with **Netflix**, which evolved from a DVD rental service to a streaming giant by embracing change and letting go of old ideas. Successful founders must stay agile and be willing to pivot their approach when the landscape changes—otherwise, they might end up as relics of a bygone era.

A related point is to **prioritize sustainable growth over meteoric rise**. The allure of rapid expansion can be intoxicating, but it often leads to decisions that compromise long-term viability. The mantra of "growth at all costs" is akin to a sugar high; it might feel great at first, but the crash can be brutal. Just look at **Uber**—despite its massive valuation and rapid growth, its aggressive tactics led to legal issues, a toxic workplace culture, and reputational damage. Sustainable growth strategies involve careful planning, market research, and a focus on profitability, rather than reckless pursuit of market share.

Lastly, the importance of **customer-centric thinking** cannot be overstated. Founders often get so wrapped up in their vision that they forget to listen to their customers. Take **MySpace**, for example. Once the king of social media, they became complacent and didn't adapt to the changing needs of their users, allowing **Facebook** to swoop in and take their throne. By staying attuned to customer feedback and evolving accordingly, founders can ensure they're meeting actual needs rather than just their own grand visions.

In summary, the tales of founder failures serve as stark reminders that charisma, vision, and ambition are essential—but they are not enough to build a sustainable business. By diversifying leadership, promoting transparency, embracing adaptability, prioritizing sustainable growth, and focusing on customer needs, future entrepreneurs can steer clear of the pitfalls that have brought down so many before them. So, let's take these lessons to heart and create a startup landscape that champions resilience and responsibility over myth and martyrdom.

The Customer Acquisition Trap: Discounting to Death

In the chaotic world of startups, one thing is clear: acquiring customers is a make-or-break endeavor. We'll explore how many businesses have fallen into a perilous cycle of discounting that ultimately leads to their demise.

At first glance, offering discounts and promotions might seem like a smart strategy—who doesn't love a good deal? Startups often view these tactics as a quick fix to attract attention and build a customer base. However, in this race to lure customers in with enticing offers, many founders neglect to consider the long-term consequences of their discounting frenzy.

This chapter will unravel the seductive nature of discounting as a customer acquisition strategy. We'll look at how this practice can create a dangerous dependence on temporary incentives rather than fostering genuine loyalty. It's a trap that, once entered, can be hard to escape.

What starts as a vibrant, customer-centric approach can quickly devolve into a grim reality where profit margins shrink, brand value diminishes, and the overall sustainability of the business hangs in the balance.

As we delve deeper, we'll examine how the allure of immediate gains can overshadow the necessity for a robust, lasting relationship with customers. We'll analyze how this discount-driven mindset often results in a revolving door of customers who are only interested in the next deal, leaving companies scrambling to find new ways to entice them back through the door.

Through case studies and real-world examples, we'll expose the stark reality of discounting to death, demonstrating that while short-term sales spikes might seem appealing, they can lead to long-term damage that far outweighs any initial benefit. By the end of this chapter, you'll understand why chasing after customer acquisition through discounting is like trying to catch smoke with your bare hands—impossible and ultimately, deeply frustrating.

Discounting as a Strategy: Short-Term Gains

Let's get into the seductive world of discounting as a strategy for customer acquisition, which at first glance feels like a golden ticket to sales success. Imagine you've just launched your shiny new startup, and you're eager to attract customers like moths to a flame. You decide to offer hefty discounts—50% off your product for the first month! It sounds great, right? You're essentially saying, "Hey, look over here! We're the best thing since sliced bread!"

Initially, this strategy can lead to an exhilarating spike in sales. You see those numbers climb, and the excitement is palpable. Everyone loves a bargain, and you feel like a marketing genius. But hold up! This initial boost can be as fleeting as a good hair day in a rainstorm.

Take the example of **Groupon**, the daily deal website that seemed to have the world at its feet for a while. Groupon's strategy relied heavily on offering steep discounts to draw in new customers for local businesses. Sure, their revenue numbers looked impressive at first, but many businesses found themselves trapped in a cycle of discounting.

While the initial influx of customers might have been delightful, the long-term implications were often disastrous. Businesses that relied on Groupon discounts saw their profit margins evaporate, and many struggled to retain customers once the deals ended. Once those discounts were gone, the customers vanished like a magician's rabbit, leaving behind a sad, empty hat.

Now, let's talk about **Blue Apron**, the meal kit delivery service that once enjoyed immense popularity. They lured in new subscribers with significant discounts for their first few deliveries. The allure of fresh ingredients and easy recipes attracted customers faster than you could say "gourmet." However, as they faced stiff competition, Blue Apron found themselves slashing prices more and more to retain customers. This led to a decline in their overall perceived value, and their financial health took a nosedive. They ended up in a vicious cycle of discounting to keep customers, but once the allure of the discounted meal kits wore off, many subscribers churned. Their once-promising business model began to crumble under the weight of their own pricing strategy.

Now, let's not forget **Zulily**, the online retailer known for offering daily deals on clothing and household items. Zulily built a significant customer base on discounts, enticing shoppers with "limited-time offers." But here's the kicker: while customers loved the deals, Zulily struggled to foster genuine loyalty. When the discounts stopped coming, many shoppers simply moved on to the next discount site. They had trained their customer base to expect sales, and once the sales dried up, so did the traffic. Zulily's dependency on discounting not only hurt their margins but also made it challenging to sustain long-term growth.

First up, **Jet.com**, the online retailer that once promised to take on Amazon. They initially attracted customers with significant discounts and unique pricing strategies, like offering lower prices when customers added more items to their cart. It worked like a charm for a while, leading to impressive user growth. However, the reliance on discounts created a culture of bargain-hunters who weren't loyal to the brand. As Jet.com attempted to scale, they realized that maintaining these discounts was not sustainable. They had to sell their business to Walmart, which struggled to integrate Jet's model into its operations.

Instead of becoming a formidable competitor, Jet.com became a cautionary tale of how discounting can lure in customers but fail to build long-term loyalty.

Let's look at **Yelp**. In its early days, Yelp offered hefty discounts and deals through its platform to encourage users to try new local businesses. While this brought in a flood of users, many businesses quickly found that customers would only come back if there was a deal on the table. Yelp had inadvertently trained its user base to seek out discounts rather than genuine value. Over time, the sheer volume of discounts diluted the brand's credibility, and many business owners became disillusioned, leading to complaints about the effectiveness of Yelp's advertising. Yelp's model turned into a revolving door of promotions and transient customers, causing long-term harm to both their platform and the businesses they aimed to support.

Let's not forget about **MoviePass**, which went through a meteoric rise thanks to its initial discount offering. They started with a model that allowed subscribers to see one movie per day for a mere $9.95 a month. It seemed too good to be true—and it was. While the initial surge in subscriptions brought in a flood of cash, MoviePass soon realized that they were effectively subsidizing ticket prices and losing massive amounts of money with every movie ticket sold. As they tried to manage the financial disaster, they began imposing restrictions, such as limiting the number of movies per month and increasing subscription prices, alienating their loyal customer base. The once-beloved brand plummeted into chaos, ultimately leading to bankruptcy. Their strategy of discounting turned a promising concept into a cautionary tale.

Then we have **Uber**, the ride-sharing giant. When Uber first entered markets, it offered steep discounts to lure in riders. While this strategy helped them gain market share, it created a user expectation for low fares that could not be sustained. Riders became accustomed to discounted rides, leading Uber to face pressure to continually drop prices or offer promotions. This discount-driven growth contributed to their ongoing financial struggles and losses. Uber found itself in a perpetual cycle of discounting to attract and retain customers while simultaneously facing massive losses.

And let's talk about **Groupon** again—yes, we can't escape this train wreck. Groupon had so many merchants who tried to offer discounts just to get customers through their doors, thinking that it would generate repeat business. However, many of these businesses learned that the customers they attracted were primarily there for the discount, not the experience. Once the coupon was used, they often never returned. This model not only hurt local businesses but also put Groupon in hot water with its merchant partners. The heavy reliance on discounting turned Groupon from a promising startup into a company struggling to redefine its value proposition and business model.

Lastly, there's **HTC**, which dominated the smartphone market in the early 2010s. They began slashing prices to combat increasing competition, especially from Apple and Samsung. While this move attracted bargain-hunting customers, it led to a significant decline in brand prestige and profit margins. As they rushed to the discount table, their smartphones began to lose value in consumers' eyes. Their market share dwindled, and by 2018, they announced significant layoffs and a strategic pivot away from smartphones. They had trained their consumers to associate the HTC brand with discounts, which ultimately hurt their long-term reputation and sustainability.

These examples illustrate that while discounting can create short-term spikes in customer acquisition, the long-term implications often lead to eroded brand value, unsustainable financial practices, and ultimately, a fragile business model. Companies that rely heavily on discounts often find themselves in a precarious position, chasing a quick fix rather than fostering real loyalty and sustainable growth. In this twisted game of customer acquisition, the thrill of discounts might quickly turn into a costly mistake, leaving companies stranded in a cycle of despair.

So, while the immediate rewards of discounting can feel thrilling, this strategy often leads to a precarious business environment where companies are forced to constantly chase the next sale. What's worse? This race to the bottom erodes brand equity, making it harder to charge premium prices later on. In the end, discounting might deliver a quick win, but it's often at the cost of long-term viability. As the saying goes, "All that glitters is not gold," and in the world of discounting, that glitter can quickly turn into rust.

The Pitfalls of a Discount-Driven Market

Companies may find themselves trapped in a vicious cycle of discounting, which erodes brand value, diminishes profit margins, and creates a fickle customer base. Take **Zulily**, the online retailer specializing in children's and women's apparel. Zulily built its brand around flash sales and deep discounts, attracting millions of users looking for the next great deal. Initially, this strategy was a hit, with sales soaring and customer acquisition rates skyrocketing. However, over time, as the novelty of constant discounts wore off, the company struggled to retain customers who had become accustomed to waiting for sales. As loyal customers shifted to other platforms, Zulily faced declining sales. They became trapped in a cycle of discounting to drive traffic, which in turn squeezed profit margins and made it increasingly challenging to sustain operations. Eventually, Zulily had to re-evaluate its business model, but the damage was already done, and the brand struggled to regain its former glory.

Another poignant example is **Sephora**, the cosmetics giant. While Sephora does offer discounts during major sales events, they also heavily rely on their loyalty program, which offers rewards for purchases. While this strategy has its merits, there's a fine line between loyalty and discounting. Some customers began to game the system, only shopping during sales events to maximize their rewards. Instead of fostering genuine brand loyalty, Sephora found itself in a position where they had to continually increase the value of discounts to keep customers engaged. As a result, they risked eroding their profit margins while consumers began to view Sephora as just another brand offering deals rather than a premium experience. This created a precarious situation for the company, as maintaining brand prestige became increasingly difficult.

Now let's look at **Warby Parker**, the trendy eyewear brand. They initially captured the market with their unique home try-on model, allowing customers to sample frames for free before purchasing. But as competitors entered the space with aggressive discounting, Warby Parker felt the heat. They eventually began to offer discounts to stay competitive. This tactic worked in the short term, attracting price-sensitive customers, but it blurred the lines of their premium positioning. Warby Parker faced the risk of diluting its brand identity by succumbing to the discount-driven mentality that dominated the eyewear market. The challenge was maintaining a balance between customer acquisition and brand value—a struggle that many companies fail to navigate successfully.

Let's not forget **Blue Apron**, the meal kit delivery service that once was the darling of the startup world. Blue Apron initially lured customers in with hefty discounts on their first few orders. While this created a surge in subscriptions, the company quickly discovered that most customers were simply interested in the discount rather than the value of the meal kits themselves. As a result, they faced staggering churn rates—customers would sign up, use their discounts, and then cancel after a few meals. This led Blue Apron to continually offer deeper discounts just to attract new subscribers. Over time, they found themselves struggling to maintain a sustainable business model, culminating in a tumultuous IPO and ongoing financial challenges. Their reliance on discounts, rather than fostering a genuine connection with their customers, ultimately hampered their long-term viability.

Then there's **J.C. Penney**, a classic case study in the dangers of discount-driven strategies. The retailer tried to abandon its reliance on coupons and discounts under former CEO Ron Johnson, shifting to an everyday low-price model. However, this move confused customers who had been conditioned to expect frequent sales. As they returned to the store expecting deals, the lack of discounts led to a massive decline in sales. J.C. Penney had to backtrack and reintroduce discounts, but by then, the damage was done. The brand struggled to recover, and it faced severe financial repercussions. This example highlights the inherent risks of a discount-driven strategy, as customer expectations can change dramatically, leading to a vicious cycle of trying to appease them.

Consider **Groupon**, yet again—a poster child for discount pitfalls. Initially, Groupon thrived by offering significant discounts to local businesses. However, as businesses grew wary of the unsustainable model, they found that the customers who came in through Groupon deals rarely returned for full-priced offerings. This trend hurt businesses financially and eroded trust in the Groupon model. The company itself began to face a decline in revenue, leading to layoffs and a substantial drop in stock value. Groupon's original value proposition turned into a liability, as the constant need for discounts created a toxic environment for both merchants and customers.

Finally, we can't ignore the story of **Lyft**. Like Uber, Lyft initially drew customers in with discounted rides to compete in a fierce market. However, this strategy resulted in a race to the bottom. With constant discounting, both companies found themselves under immense financial pressure. Lyft had to spend heavily on subsidies to keep customers engaged, which hurt their bottom line. As they struggled to differentiate themselves, their brand identity became entangled in the discount-driven narrative, impacting their ability to establish long-term loyalty. Lyft's reliance on short-term gains ultimately hindered its profitability and growth potential.

These case studies clearly illustrate that while discounting can provide an initial surge in customer acquisition, it often leads to more significant long-term challenges. In the end, the excitement of temporary gains can lead to a host of pitfalls that hinder sustainable growth and long-term success. In this game, the allure of discounts often transforms into a haunting ghost, lurking behind every business decision, ready to strike when least expected.

A classic tale of discounting gone awry is the case of **Kraft Heinz**. Once a behemoth in the food industry, the company faced intense competition from healthier, organic brands. In an attempt to retain market share, Kraft Heinz resorted to aggressive discounting on its processed food products. While this strategy attracted price-sensitive customers, it ultimately led to a devaluation of their brand. Consumers began to perceive Kraft products as cheap alternatives rather than the quality offerings they once were. The long-term implication? Sales continued to decline, and the company had to grapple with the consequences of a tarnished reputation. In a race to compete on price, they forgot that branding is as much about perception as it is about profit.

Another striking example is **The Gap**. Once a trendy retailer, The Gap attempted to boost sales by slashing prices and running constant sales promotions. While this brought in foot traffic, the company soon found that customers were no longer willing to pay full price. The brand began to lose its cachet, and the relentless discounting led to an identity crisis. The Gap found itself in a position where it was struggling to attract customers at regular prices, resulting in declining revenues. The perception of the brand shifted from fashionable to merely a place for bargains, ultimately jeopardizing its long-term health.

Sears is another sobering example of a discount trap. The once-giant retailer tried to stay relevant in an evolving retail landscape by offering heavy discounts on its products. Initially, this strategy worked, but it soon backfired. As consumers flocked to Sears for deals, the company found itself trapped in a cycle of discounting that eroded its profit margins. The result? A deterioration of brand loyalty, as customers began to associate Sears with low prices rather than quality products. Eventually, the relentless discounting couldn't save Sears from bankruptcy, highlighting how a short-term focus can lead to long-term demise.

Let's not forget **RadioShack**. The electronics retailer desperately tried to stay afloat by offering steep discounts on its products. Initially, this approach drew in customers, but the constant promotions devalued the brand and created an image of desperation. As competitors like Best Buy and Amazon emerged, RadioShack found itself unable to compete on price while still delivering value. The discount-driven model became unsustainable, leading to a downward spiral that culminated in bankruptcy. RadioShack's reliance on discounts proved to be a double-edged sword, ultimately cutting deep into its viability.

Then there's the infamous **American Apparel**. Known for its provocative marketing and trendy apparel, American Apparel initially captured a niche market. However, as competition increased, the brand resorted to aggressive discounting to entice customers. This approach led to a significant decline in profit margins and brand prestige. American Apparel struggled to maintain its image as a quality brand while constantly offering discounts, which ultimately resulted in a financial crisis. The over-reliance on discounts eroded customer loyalty, leading to a series of missteps that contributed to its bankruptcy.

Let's take a look at **Jet.com**, the e-commerce platform founded by Marc Lore. Jet.com launched with an innovative pricing model that offered discounts based on how customers shopped. However, as the competition heated up with Amazon's massive scale and logistical capabilities, Jet began to offer steeper discounts to attract customers. This led to unsustainable operating losses and a lack of differentiation in the market. While Jet was eventually acquired by Walmart, the discount-driven strategy led to a struggle to establish a unique brand identity and profitability. It serves as a reminder that trying to out-discount competitors can often backfire, creating a race to the bottom rather than a path to sustainable growth.

We should also mention **Shutterfly**. The personalized photo services company thrived on seasonal discounts and promotions. However, as competitors emerged with similar offerings, Shutterfly was forced to ramp up its discounting strategies to maintain market share. While this approach initially boosted customer acquisition, it quickly became apparent that the long-term implications were dire. Shutterfly's profit margins dwindled, and the brand began to lose its premium positioning. Customers began to wait for the next sale rather than engaging with the brand at full price, leading to an unsustainable business model. The over-reliance on discounts ultimately jeopardized Shutterfly's financial health.

Finally, let's discuss **Fiverr**, the online marketplace for freelance services. Fiverr initially attracted a large customer base with its $5 gigs, creating a perception of affordability. However, as competitors like Upwork and Freelancer entered the market, Fiverr felt compelled to keep its pricing low. This led to a discount-driven culture where freelancers were pressured to lower their rates to attract buyers. The result was a devaluation of services and a struggle for many freelancers to make a sustainable income. Fiverr's initial promise of connecting clients with affordable talent devolved into a race to the bottom, where quality was sacrificed at the altar of discounting. This illustrates how an initial successful strategy can lead to long-term pitfalls when it relies too heavily on discounts.

In summary, these examples paint a vivid picture of the pitfalls inherent in a discount-driven market. While discounts can create short-term customer acquisition wins, they often lead to long-term challenges such as eroded brand value, diminished profit margins, and a fickle customer base. Companies can find themselves caught in a relentless cycle of discounting that ultimately jeopardizes their sustainability and growth. In this game, relying solely on discounts can lead to a legacy of regret, with brands left wondering how they let themselves be swept away in a tide of short-term gains that left them stranded in the long run.

The Challenge of Building Customer Loyalty

Building customer loyalty in a discount-driven market is like trying to build a sandcastle at low tide: no matter how impressive your structure looks at first, it's bound to wash away when the next wave comes crashing in. When companies rely solely on discounts to attract customers, they create a transactional relationship rather than fostering genuine loyalty. Let's delve into some eye-opening examples that illustrate this challenge.

Take **J.C. Penney**, for instance. The retail giant decided to overhaul its pricing strategy by eliminating sales and discounts altogether, opting for "everyday low prices." They aimed to cultivate a sense of trust and transparency with customers. However, the loyal customer base had been conditioned to expect sales and discounts for so long that they were unwilling to adapt. Sales plummeted, and J.C. Penney had to backtrack, proving that when customers are trained to expect discounts, shifting gears is like steering a ship in a storm—practically impossible.

Another classic example is **Groupon**, which built its brand on daily deals and discounts. While it initially drew in millions of users, the reliance on steep discounts meant that customers often viewed the service as a means to snag a bargain rather than a platform for valuable offerings. Merchants participating in Groupon promotions quickly realized that they were often seen as the "cheap option," which undermined brand loyalty. When the deals disappeared, so did the customers, revealing how discount-driven engagement can be fleeting at best.

Old Navy is another cautionary tale. Known for its vibrant marketing and frequent sales, Old Navy heavily leaned on discounts to drive foot traffic. While this strategy worked in the short term, it created a scenario where customers became accustomed to waiting for sales before making purchases. The brand's identity shifted from one of quality and style to simply being "the place with good deals." As a result, customer loyalty dwindled, and many shoppers opted to shop elsewhere once they felt they could get similar styles at discounted prices.

Let's not overlook **Bonobos**, which initially gained traction with its innovative online shopping model and great customer service. However, as competitors flooded the market, Bonobos resorted to discounts to keep up. While they did attract new customers, the brand found itself in a precarious position, with a customer base that was more interested in snagging a deal than becoming loyal advocates. The once-dedicated customers became indifferent, as their focus shifted to price rather than brand values. This challenge is a classic example of how discounting can dilute a brand's identity and its ability to foster true loyalty.

The case of **Zulily** illustrates how a discount-centric model can impact customer loyalty. This online retailer specializes in flash sales and steep discounts, attracting bargain-hunters looking for unique items. However, the company struggled to retain customers long-term, as shoppers often left for better deals elsewhere. Loyalty programs and personalized marketing efforts fell flat because customers were primarily motivated by price, not brand connection. Zulily's discount-driven model made it challenging to cultivate a loyal customer base that returned for reasons beyond the latest sale.

Blue Apron also faced similar hurdles when it entered the meal kit delivery space. Initially, the company attracted a customer base eager to try new recipes at a discount. However, as competitors emerged with more innovative offerings, Blue Apron felt compelled to discount its prices. Over time, this tactic undermined its perceived value, and customers became increasingly disengaged. Loyalty dwindled as consumers hopped from one meal kit service to another, driven solely by pricing rather than brand loyalty or a commitment to the Blue Apron experience.

Even **Kohl's**, known for its ubiquitous coupons and discounts, faced challenges in building lasting customer loyalty. The retailer relied heavily on promotional strategies to draw in shoppers, creating a scenario where many customers only visited the store during sales. This reliance on discounts diluted the brand's value, leading customers to feel that shopping at Kohl's was more about scoring a deal than appreciating the products. When Kohl's tried to shift away from its discount-driven model, many customers resisted, revealing just how difficult it is to break the cycle once it's established.

Finally, let's examine **Panda Express**. The fast-casual restaurant chain often offers discounts and promotions to entice customers. While this strategy boosts short-term sales, it creates a scenario where many customers come for the deals but don't develop a lasting affinity for the brand. The challenge is exacerbated by the sheer volume of competitors in the fast-casual space, making it difficult for Panda Express to establish a unique brand identity that goes beyond promotional offerings.

In conclusion, building customer loyalty in a discount-driven market is no small feat. The fleeting nature of discounts can create transactional relationships rather than long-lasting connections, leaving companies grappling with the challenge of retaining customers who are more interested in getting a deal than being loyal to a brand. As we've seen from various case studies, the over-reliance on discounts can undermine a company's identity, erode brand value, and create a fickle customer base. In this dynamic, businesses must find a balance between attracting customers with appealing offers and fostering genuine loyalty that transcends mere price considerations. Otherwise, they risk becoming yet another casualty in the relentless tide of discount-driven consumerism.

The Long-Term Effects of Constant Discounting

Constant discounting can have a range of long-term effects on businesses that extend well beyond the immediate spike in sales. It's like putting a band-aid on a bullet wound; it might seem like a good fix at first, but eventually, the underlying issues start to fester. Let's explore the various long-term repercussions of a discount-driven strategy through some relevant examples and case studies.

First off, one of the most significant long-term effects is the **erosion of brand value**. When customers become accustomed to discounts, the perceived value of a brand diminishes. This was evident with **Sears**, once a retail giant known for its quality products. As it began to rely heavily on discounts and sales, the brand's identity shifted from that of a trusted retailer to a bargain store. Customers started to associate Sears with low prices rather than quality or reliability, leading to a steep decline in brand loyalty and ultimately contributing to the company's downfall.

Another key impact is the **increased price sensitivity** among customers. When discounting becomes the norm, shoppers will often wait for sales before making purchases, conditioning them to only buy at reduced prices. Take **Macy's**, for instance. The department store chain frequently employs deep discounting to drive foot traffic. While this tactic temporarily boosts sales, it has led to a customer base that is hyper-aware of sales cycles. This resulted in many shoppers delaying their purchases, waiting for the next big sale. This habit is detrimental to sales during non-discount periods, making it challenging for the brand to maintain consistent revenue.

Let's also consider the **profit margin squeeze**. Relying on discounts to drive sales often means lower profit margins. While companies may see a surge in sales volume, the reality is that many of them end up sacrificing profitability. This is exemplified by **Groupon**, which attracted millions of users with its discount deals. However, as merchants began to see diminishing returns from the high discounts, many opted out of the platform. Groupon's model, built on discounting, became unsustainable, leading to financial struggles and an eventual decline in market value. The company's aggressive discounting strategy came at the expense of long-term sustainability and profitability.

Then there's the **challenge of customer retention**. In a discount-driven market, customer loyalty is often superficial. For example, when **J.C. Penney** attempted to shift away from its deep discounting strategy to an "everyday low price" model, it struggled to retain customers who had been conditioned to only shop during sales. The result was a dramatic drop in revenue as the loyal customer base had become accustomed to the thrill of scoring deals rather than building an emotional connection with the brand. This demonstrated how discounting can lead to fickle customer relationships that are hard to rebuild.

Market positioning also suffers in a discount-driven landscape. Brands that are known for constant discounts may find it difficult to reposition themselves as premium or high-quality options in the future. A prime example is **Old Navy**, which became known for its frequent sales and promotions. This approach not only reduced the perceived quality of its offerings but also made it challenging for the brand to pivot back to a strategy focused on quality over discounts. When customers associate a brand with bargains, it's an uphill battle to change that perception, making it tough for the brand to capture a different segment of the market.

Moreover, businesses may become **over-reliant on discounts as a marketing strategy**, leading to a cycle that's hard to break. For instance, **Zulily** built its entire brand on flash sales and deep discounts. While this brought in initial success, it left little room for creativity or innovation in customer engagement. As competition increased, Zulily struggled to maintain its foothold in the market. The company's reliance on constant discounting made it difficult to differentiate itself, leading to stagnation and a loss of market share.

Finally, there's the **negative impact on employee morale and brand culture**. When a company constantly promotes discounts, it can create a culture where employees feel pressured to sell at lower prices, which can be demoralizing. This is particularly true in the retail sector, where employees may feel their efforts are undervalued when customers are only focused on getting the best deal. For instance, at **Kohl's**, sales associates often feel like they're stuck in a cycle of discounting, which can lead to job dissatisfaction and high turnover rates. A brand's culture, after all, should embody the values and quality that they want their customers to associate with them.

In conclusion, the long-term effects of constant discounting extend beyond immediate sales boosts and can damage a brand's identity, profitability, and customer relationships. As businesses prioritize short-term gains through discounts, they risk losing sight of what truly matters: building a loyal customer base, maintaining brand integrity, and ensuring long-term sustainability. Brands that recognize the pitfalls of a discount-driven model can pivot to a more balanced strategy that emphasizes value and quality, fostering genuine customer loyalty in the process. Otherwise, they may find themselves trapped in a cycle of fleeting sales and diminishing returns.

Case Studies of Companies That Failed

When it comes to the long-term effects of discount-driven strategies, several high-profile case studies exemplify how discounting can lead to a downward spiral. These companies didn't just stumble; they spectacularly collapsed under the weight of their own discounting practices. Let's take a closer look at some of these cautionary tales.

1. J.C. Penney: Once a staple of American retail, J.C. Penney attempted to revitalize its brand by moving away from a culture of deep discounting in 2011. Under the leadership of then-CEO Ron

Johnson, the company introduced a pricing strategy that favored "everyday low prices" rather than frequent sales and discounts. Unfortunately, this shift backfired spectacularly. Customers who had been conditioned to wait for sales were not ready to embrace this new approach. As a result, sales plummeted, and the company suffered significant financial losses. J.C. Penney's attempt to shed its discount-driven identity not only failed to attract new customers but alienated its existing ones, leading to a bankruptcy filing in 2020.

2. Sears: Another classic example, Sears was once an iconic retailer in the U.S., known for its quality and reliability. Over the years, the company increasingly relied on deep discounts to drive foot traffic. However, this reliance on promotions eroded its brand value. By the time it realized the damage done, it was too late. Sears became synonymous with clearance sales rather than quality products. The brand lost customer loyalty, leading to a decline in market share, and eventually, the company filed for bankruptcy in 2018. The collapse was a glaring example of how discounting can lead to a brand's downfall when it becomes the primary selling point.

3. Groupon: Initially a darling of the startup world, Groupon's business model revolved around offering massive discounts on local services and products. While this attracted a vast customer base at first, the model proved unsustainable. Merchants quickly realized that the discounts were cutting too deeply into their profits. As many businesses began to opt-out of the platform, Groupon struggled to retain customers and merchants alike. By focusing primarily on discounts, Groupon created a cycle of diminishing returns, ultimately leading to a significant decline in its stock price and market relevance. Today, it stands as a case study of how a discount-driven model can quickly unravel.

4. Old Navy: This brand, part of the Gap Inc. portfolio, became known for its frequent sales and constant discounting. While Old Navy initially enjoyed success with this strategy, it eventually diluted the brand's value. Customers became accustomed to shopping only during sales events, which made it difficult for the brand to maintain consistent pricing and profitability. In an effort to pivot back to a more balanced pricing strategy, Old Navy has struggled to reclaim its former identity and customer loyalty. Its case illustrates how being too reliant on discounts can ultimately erode brand equity and consumer trust.

5. The Children's Place: This retailer also fell into the trap of discounting. Originally focused on children's apparel, The Children's Place employed a heavy discounting strategy to compete in a crowded market. While this tactic initially increased sales, it also led to a reduction in profitability. The brand became known for its discounts rather than quality, and as a result, it struggled to differentiate itself from competitors. The long-term consequences included a decline in sales, layoffs, and store closures as the company sought to adjust its strategy.

6. RadioShack: Once a go-to destination for electronic gadgets and accessories, RadioShack relied heavily on constant promotions and discounts to drive sales. As technology rapidly evolved, the brand failed to innovate and adapt, choosing instead to compete primarily on price. Eventually, its discount-driven model alienated consumers seeking quality and service. The culmination of these strategies resulted in a significant decline in market presence, leading to the company filing for bankruptcy twice, in 2015 and 2017. RadioShack serves as a warning of how discounting can overshadow innovation and brand integrity.

These case studies underline the dangers of a discount-driven approach. While discounting can drive short-term gains, it often leads to long-term consequences that can cripple a brand's identity, profitability, and overall market position. The cycle of relying on discounts can diminish perceived value, create price sensitivity, and foster an environment where customer loyalty becomes fleeting. These companies learned the hard way that a strategy based solely on discounting can ultimately lead to their undoing.

The IPO Mirage: Going Public Without Profits

The glitzy red carpets, the ticker symbols flashing on Wall Street, and the promise of untold riches. But let's be real for a second: going public without turning a profit is like throwing a massive party in your parents' basement while claiming you're a financial guru. Spoiler alert: the balloons won't hide the fact that you still owe your buddy twenty bucks.

In this chapter, we're diving deep into the dazzling yet deceptive realm of IPOs. You see, some companies rush to go public like a kid racing to the ice cream truck, all while ignoring the fact that they've been running on fumes and fancy financial gymnastics rather than solid fundamentals. Sure, they may have the flashy growth metrics and the social media buzz, but when it comes down to it, are they truly viable businesses?

Take Uber, for instance. It burst onto the public scene with all the flair of a rockstar but had never actually turned a profit. Instead, it relied on investors' hopes and dreams to fuel its relentless pursuit of growth. And guess what? That didn't exactly set the stage for a smooth ride. Companies like WeWork took the stage too, flaunting high valuations and big ambitions, only to stumble spectacularly when the curtain was pulled back, revealing a shaky foundation.

As we explore this chapter, we'll uncover the illusion of success that surrounds IPOs, highlighting the risks of chasing hype instead of real-world results. After all, who needs profits when you can have a million-dollar valuation? Just remember: in the world of IPOs, appearances can be deceiving, and the real magic lies in sustainable growth, not just a dazzling launch. So, let's pop that champagne and take a closer look at the IPO mirage—because it's about to get interesting!

IPOs: The Illusion of Success

Ah, the IPO: the grand spectacle where companies dress up like they're headed to the prom, hoping the world will believe they're ready for the big leagues. It's all about that initial public offering, baby! You get to ring the bell, bask in the spotlight, and watch your stock price skyrocket—until it doesn't, and you're left picking up the pieces like an awkward teen after the dance.

Let's talk about the illusion of success surrounding IPOs. Companies like Uber and WeWork strutted into the public eye like they owned the place, but underneath all that swagger was a shaky foundation built on hopes, dreams, and a dash of desperation. Uber, for example, went public in 2019, sporting a valuation of $82 billion. Sounds fantastic, right? Until you realize they had never turned a profit. That's like throwing a birthday party for yourself but forgetting to invite any friends. You might have the cake and candles, but good luck celebrating alone!

Then there's WeWork, which took the term "hot mess" to a whole new level. With a valuation that peaked at $47 billion, it felt like a tech fairy tale. But behind the scenes, the company was a ticking time bomb of poor management and questionable business practices. Their highly publicized IPO attempt crashed and burned faster than a toddler on a sugar high. WeWork's story serves as a cautionary tale: sometimes, the people who seem the most confident are just good at putting on a show while hiding a complete disaster behind the curtain.

And let's not forget about the phenomenon of "pumping and dumping." No, I'm not talking about a questionable workout routine; I'm referring to the practice where companies inflate their valuations to lure in investors, only to leave them high and dry once they've made their quick exit. It's like a magician making a rabbit disappear—only in this case, the rabbit is your investment.

Investors often fall for the flashy promises of growth metrics and "disruptive" business models, mistaking them for sound fundamentals. Spoiler alert: growth doesn't equal sustainability. Take Snap Inc., for instance. It went public with much fanfare, only to watch its stock plummet as investors realized that maybe, just maybe, a disappearing photo app wasn't a long-term strategy. In their case, the excitement of an IPO quickly faded, leaving behind the sobering reality of their financial performance—or lack thereof.

The bottom line? IPOs can create the illusion of success, but beneath the shiny surface lies a murky reality. The glitz and glam may make for great headlines, but if the underlying business isn't solid, those headline figures won't mean a damn thing. So, next time you're tempted by the bright lights of an IPO, remember: it's not about how you look in a tux; it's about whether you can dance when the music starts.

Take **Uber**, for instance. Launched in 2019 with much fanfare, it debuted at a whopping $82 billion valuation. On the surface, it seemed like a tech fairy tale come to life. But here's the kicker: Uber had never made a profit. It's akin to showing up to a potluck with an empty dish and expecting everyone to applaud your culinary skills. Uber continued to burn cash like a pyromaniac at a bonfire party, all while promising investors that growth was just around the corner. Fast forward a few years, and their stock has seen more ups and downs than a roller coaster. It's a classic case of "look at our growth!" while the financial health is teetering on the edge of a cliff.

Then there's **WeWork**, the coworking space company that thought it could disrupt the entire real estate industry. With a peak valuation of $47 billion, it looked like a unicorn ready to gallop into the sunset. But behind the scenes, it was a chaotic circus led by co-founder Adam Neumann, who seemed more interested in personal branding and chasing ambition than solid business practices. When WeWork tried to go public, investors were treated to a dumpster fire of financial disclosures that revealed losses larger than some countries' GDPs. They pulled their IPO at the last minute, and the company's valuation plummeted faster than a lead balloon. The dream of a successful IPO turned into a nightmare, showcasing the dangers of flashy promises without solid foundations.

Let's not forget **Snap Inc.**, the parent company of Snapchat. When it went public in 2017, it was hailed as a massive success with an initial valuation of around $24 billion. However, it didn't take long for reality to set in. Investors quickly realized that Snap was a platform that thrived on ephemeral content—content that disappears as soon as it's viewed. Sounds cute, right? But what happens when users grow tired of sending pictures of their lunch? Snap's stock took a nosedive as growth slowed, and profitability remained elusive. It's like opening a bakery that only sells cupcakes on Tuesdays—great idea, but if you can't keep up the variety, you'll find yourself with a lot of stale treats.

Then we have **Peloton**, the at-home fitness company that rode the pandemic wave to great heights. With an IPO valuation of about $8 billion, it seemed like they could do no wrong—until they did. As gyms reopened and the world began to move again, Peloton's growth stalled, and they were left with a warehouse full of overpriced exercise bikes gathering dust. The stock plummeted, and the once-hyped unicorn found itself grappling with a fading business model and an abundance of unsold inventory. Turns out, people prefer a leisurely bike ride to sweating it out in their living rooms when the weather is nice.

Lastly, consider **Lyft**, Uber's main competitor. Lyft's IPO was celebrated as a milestone for the ride-sharing industry, but it quickly became apparent that it was just a glorified ticket to the financial circus. With a debut valuation of $24 billion and the promise of disrupting transportation, investors were excited—until they weren't. Lyft also failed to show a profit, and its stock fell below its initial pricing within months. It was like watching a magician pull a rabbit out of a hat only for the rabbit to be a stuffed toy.

These examples paint a clear picture of how the allure of IPOs can often mask deeper issues. They're like the shiny wrapping on a poorly made gift—pretty on the outside but lacking any substance on the inside. The hype surrounding these companies can create an illusion of success, leading investors to believe they're buying into the next big thing, when in reality, they might just be falling for a well-crafted mirage.

The Rush to Go Public

The rush to go public is like that moment when you're waiting for your favorite band to drop their new album, and suddenly you see a notification pop up: "Pre-order now!" It's a thrill ride, and everyone wants a piece of the action. But let's be real—going public isn't just a victory lap; it's more like jumping on a speeding train with a blindfold on, hoping you don't end up face-first in a pile of financial regret.

Let's start with **Robinhood**, the trading app that came to fame by democratizing stock trading. The hype was palpable leading up to its IPO in 2021. They promised the revolution of investing—who wouldn't want to be a part of that? However, the reality behind the curtain was far less glamorous. Just days before their public debut, they faced legal troubles related to their business practices, and investors were left scratching their heads, wondering if this was a sign of a tumultuous ride ahead. Spoiler alert: it was! The stock plummeted post-IPO, proving that sometimes, it's better to take your time and make sure the train is on the right track before you jump aboard.

Then there's **OYO Rooms**, the Indian hospitality startup that tried to disrupt the hotel industry. In 2019, the company announced plans for an IPO, painting a rosy picture of growth and expansion. Investors were chomping at the bit, lured by the prospect of a billion-dollar valuation. But beneath the shiny surface was a different story—OYO was grappling with financial woes, and many of its properties were in dire straits. The rush to go public was more about maintaining an image than actually delivering on promises. When OYO eventually filed for its IPO, it was clear that the hype train had derailed, with the company needing to re-evaluate its strategy amid concerns over its sustainability.

And let's not overlook **Kraft Heinz**. In 2015, this food giant merged with Kraft to create a culinary behemoth. They were riding high on the success of their initial public offering, but things quickly soured. The company rushed to acquire brands at breakneck speed, with little attention to integration and operational efficiency. Fast forward to 2019, and Kraft Heinz found itself writing down the value of several of its brands by billions, sending its stock tumbling. Investors were left feeling like they had been duped into a buy-one-get-one-free scheme—only to discover they got a faulty product instead.

A more recent example is **BuzzFeed**, the media company that tried to pivot from viral quizzes to a solid revenue model. BuzzFeed went public through a SPAC (Special Purpose Acquisition Company) in 2021, generating buzz and excitement about their "media empire." However, the reality was far less glamorous, with the company's stock price plummeting shortly after its debut. Investors quickly realized that the once-mighty media darling was struggling to monetize its audience, leaving many feeling like they had just signed up for a free trial that was anything but free.

In each of these cases, the rush to go public highlights a critical truth: just because you can, doesn't mean you should. Companies often feel the pressure to go public to satisfy investors, raise funds, and create a sense of legitimacy. But in doing so, they risk glossing over significant operational challenges and financial realities. It's like throwing a party and inviting everyone without cleaning up the mess in your living room first. Sure, it may look like a blast from the outside, but once the guests start to notice the chaos, you might find yourself cleaning up more than just spilled drinks.

So, the next time you hear about a company making headlines with an IPO, remember: behind the glitz and glam, there's often a rush that can lead to a crash, proving that the race to go public is not always a sprint to success but sometimes a mad dash into uncertainty.

Post-IPO Struggles: A Harsh Reality

Welcome to the post-IPO party, where the confetti has fallen, and the champagne has gone flat. Just like that friend who insists they can drink everyone under the table at the bar, many companies often stumble after going public. The truth is, the IPO was just the opening act, and what comes next can be a reality check of epic proportions.

Take **WeWork**, for example. When WeWork announced its intention to go public in 2019, they painted an image of a thriving shared workspace revolution. Investors were lured by promises of growth and innovation—who wouldn't want a piece of the office of the future? But as the IPO date approached, the company's financials revealed a stark reality: they were burning cash faster than a bonfire on a chilly night. Investors quickly realized that the company was valuing itself at tens of billions while operating at a staggering loss. When the dust settled, the IPO was scrapped, and the once-cocky co-founder, Adam Neumann, found himself ousted. Talk about a crash landing!

Then we have **Snap Inc.**, the parent company of Snapchat, which went public in 2017 amid much fanfare. The stock initially soared, with investors giddy over the potential of disappearing messages. However, the excitement quickly turned sour when Snap struggled to monetize its user base and faced fierce competition from Instagram. Within a few quarters, the stock price was plummeting faster than a bad Tinder date. Snap's post-IPO struggles highlight the perils of having a flashy product without a solid revenue model. After all, a disappearing message might be cool, but disappearing profits? Not so much.

Let's also talk about **Peloton**, the fitness unicorn that saw its stock skyrocket during the pandemic as home workouts became the norm. But once the world started opening up again, the reality hit hard:

people were ready to ditch their stationary bikes for outdoor runs or a gym membership. As demand dwindled, Peloton found itself with a surplus of inventory and declining sales. The company had to make tough decisions, including layoffs and significant price cuts, to regain some semblance of stability. This classic "what goes up must come down" scenario serves as a sobering reminder that even the hottest trends can cool off faster than a summer day in the Arctic.

And let's not forget **Blue Apron**, the meal kit delivery service that was one of the first to hit the market. After a successful IPO in 2017, the company's stock quickly plunged as competition flooded the market and customer acquisition costs skyrocketed. Blue Apron struggled to retain customers and had to resort to heavy discounting to entice new sign-ups. The irony? They ended up in the exact predicament they sought to escape—the pit of discount-driven marketing. Blue Apron's story is a cautionary tale of how quickly the euphoria of an IPO can morph into a struggle for survival.

Even larger players like **Uber** have faced challenges post-IPO. After going public in 2019, the company experienced intense scrutiny over its profitability and business model. Despite its massive valuation, Uber has continually grappled with issues related to driver compensation, regulatory hurdles, and fierce competition from other ride-sharing platforms. The initial excitement of their IPO quickly turned into a reality check, with investors wondering if they were backing a winning horse or just chasing a mirage in the desert of the gig economy.

In a nutshell, the post-IPO struggles reveal that the initial hype can often mask deeper issues within a company. It's easy to get swept up in the excitement of a public offering, but as these examples show, the harsh reality often involves navigating a maze of operational challenges, financial scrutiny, and the looming threat of competition. Companies that thrive after going public are those that are not only ready for the spotlight but also have a robust business model that can withstand the scrutiny that comes with being a publicly traded entity. So, if you're thinking about riding the IPO wave, just remember: it's not all champagne and confetti. Sometimes, it's just a harsh hangover waiting to happen.

Case Studies of Failed IPOs

Failed IPOs—now that's a topic that brings out the popcorn! You might think that going public is the ultimate goal for any startup, but the harsh reality is that not every IPO is a fairy tale ending. Let's dive into some notable case studies of companies that not only stumbled during their public debut but fell flat on their faces.

1. WeWork

Ah, the poster child for an IPO disaster. WeWork's planned IPO in 2019 was akin to a magician's disappearing act—everyone was mesmerized until the curtain was pulled back. When the company initially filed for its public offering, it touted its massive valuation of $47 billion and the idea that it was revolutionizing workspaces. But as investors peeled back the layers, they discovered financial statements that looked more like a game of Jenga than a robust business model. Massive losses, a confusing governance structure, and the charismatic (some might say erratic) leadership of Adam Neumann led to investor skepticism. The company was forced to withdraw its IPO, and its valuation plummeted to just $8 billion. Instead of ringing the bell on

Wall Street, Neumann was shown the door. The lesson? Hype can only take you so far if reality has a nasty surprise in store.

2. Blue Apron

Remember the meal kit delivery craze? Well, Blue Apron was supposed to be the king of that castle. It went public in 2017 with high hopes and a valuation of nearly $2 billion. But as soon as it hit the market, the stock price dropped faster than a soggy meal kit. The company struggled to retain customers amid increasing competition and high customer acquisition costs. Within just a few months of going public, Blue Apron's stock was trading at a fraction of its IPO price, and they had to resort to desperate measures like deep discounting just to stay afloat. Fast forward to today, and Blue Apron is still grappling with profitability. The irony? They turned into exactly what they fought against—discount-driven survival tactics. Talk about a kitchen nightmare!

3. Snap Inc. (Snapchat)

Snap Inc. had investors swooning when it went public in March 2017. The stock opened at $17 and surged to $27 on the first day. But like a promising relationship that turns out to be a total dud, the initial excitement quickly fizzled. Snap failed to deliver consistent growth, and its monetization strategies faced fierce competition from Facebook and Instagram. As user growth plateaued, Snap's stock plummeted, leaving investors wondering what had just happened. From a $28 billion valuation, it took mere months for the company to experience a significant drop. In the end, Snap's journey is a stark reminder that initial excitement doesn't guarantee long-term success; it's like going on a blind date only to find out your match has a hidden collection of cat sweaters.

4. Theranos

Theranos was once the darling of Silicon Valley, boasting a $9 billion valuation based on the promise of revolutionizing blood testing. Their IPO, which never actually happened, was built on hype and secrecy. The company claimed to conduct comprehensive blood tests using just a few drops of blood, but investigations revealed the technology was largely a fraud. As the truth came out, the company crumbled, and its founder, Elizabeth Holmes, faced criminal charges for fraud. Theranos serves as a prime example of how the rush to go public without delivering on promises can lead to catastrophic failure. It's like throwing a party for your non-existent product—eventually, someone's going to call you out for being the life of the party with an empty wallet.

5. Pets.com

Ah, the infamous Pets.com! Launched during the dot-com bubble, this online pet supply retailer went public in 2000 with an absurdly high valuation. The sock puppet mascot and catchy ads made it a household name, but the business model was about as solid as a house of cards. Pets.com lost millions every quarter, and within nine months of its IPO, it was dead in the water. The lesson here? Just because you have a cute mascot doesn't mean you have a viable business. Pets.com reminds us all that sometimes, your best marketing strategy can't save you from being a glorified online pet cemetery.

These case studies serve as cautionary tales about the IPO process. Companies can generate all the hype they want, but without a sustainable business model, sound financial health, and the ability to adapt to market realities, the road to going public can quickly turn into a slippery slope. Investors and founders alike should remember: the journey doesn't end at the IPO; it's just the beginning, and the real challenge lies ahead. So, buckle up, folks!

Future of IPOs in the Startup Ecosystem

The future of IPOs in the startup ecosystem is looking like a thrilling rollercoaster ride—one filled with unexpected twists, sharp drops, and a few loop-de-loops. If the past few years have taught us anything, it's that going public is not just a shiny badge of honor; it's a test of endurance, financial acumen, and a sprinkle of luck. So, let's dive into what we can expect in the world of IPOs, all while tossing in a dose of sarcasm, wit, and maybe a pop culture reference or two.

First off, **the rise of SPACs** (Special Purpose Acquisition Companies) is a game changer. Remember when going public was all about long roadshows and traditional underwriting? Well, with the SPAC craze, companies can now bypass some of that rigmarole and get straight to the big leagues. It's like skipping the lines at Disneyland—who wouldn't want that? SPACs offer an enticing shortcut to the public markets, and while they may seem like the cool kids on the block, they come with their own set of risks. The party atmosphere can lead to hasty decisions, inflated valuations, and, let's be honest, a bit of a "who brought the weird dip?" situation. Just look at the flurry of SPACs that went public only to crash and burn because the underlying businesses weren't ready for prime time.

Next up, **the shift towards profitability** is not just a passing trend; it's a full-on renaissance. After years of "growth at all costs," investors are starting to wake up and smell the coffee (or the burnt toast, depending on your startup's situation). Companies that used to bask in their multi-billion-dollar valuations without a hint of profit are now facing a reality check. The buzzwords of the past—"disruption" and "market share"—are giving way to "sustainability" and "profit margins." It's like a group of teenagers finally realizing they can't live off instant noodles forever. Investors are looking for companies with sound business models that can weather the storms of the market, and those who continue to chase shiny growth metrics without addressing their financial health might find themselves on the outside looking in.

Then we have **the ever-evolving regulatory landscape**. With the fallout from some high-profile IPO disasters, you can bet that regulators are sharpening their pencils and taking a long, hard look at the processes that led to these debacles. Expect more scrutiny on financial disclosures, governance practices, and the ethical implications of hyperbolic marketing. It's a bit like having a parent watching your every move at a party—fun times! Companies that go public will need to ensure that their practices are transparent and responsible. Otherwise, they might find themselves in a precarious position—like trying to explain your TikTok dance moves to your grandma.

Technology will play a huge role in shaping the future of IPOs. Think about it: the way we analyze data, engage with investors, and run businesses is changing rapidly. The rise of AI and machine learning can offer insights into market trends, investor behavior, and risk assessment that were previously unattainable. In a world where data is king, companies that leverage technology will have a competitive edge. Just imagine how different the IPO process could look with predictive analytics guiding decision-making—no more crystal balls needed!

Last but not least, **the global perspective** on IPOs is shifting. The startup ecosystem is no longer confined to Silicon Valley or New York City. Cities around the globe are cultivating their own entrepreneurial ecosystems, and investors are looking beyond traditional markets. Whether it's tech hubs in India, fintech innovation in Africa, or green startups in Europe, the diversity of companies seeking public listings is expanding. It's a global marketplace out there, folks! The more diverse the pool of companies, the more exciting and unpredictable the IPO landscape will become.

In summary, the future of IPOs is a mixed bag of challenges and opportunities. As startups navigate the ever-changing market dynamics, they must adapt to new expectations, embrace transparency, and leverage technology to carve out their niche. The IPO path may be fraught with pitfalls, but for those brave enough to tackle it with a solid foundation and a keen understanding of the landscape, the rewards can be great. So buckle up and stay tuned—this ride is far from over!

Investor Exodus: When the Funding Dries Up

Picture this as the dramatic moment in a movie where the hero's fortune takes a nosedive—think of it like watching a high-stakes poker game where everyone suddenly folds, leaving our protagonist with nothing but an empty chip tray and a look of disbelief. Spoiler alert: it's not going to end well for our startup friends.

In this chapter, we're diving deep into the abyss of dwindling funding, where the glamorous facade of startup life begins to crack, revealing a chaotic scramble for cash and a crisis of confidence. After all, nothing says "success" quite like being flush with cash—until the investors suddenly pack their bags and head for the exits, leaving you with nothing but your dwindling hope and a few loyal employees trying to keep the lights on.

We'll explore the reasons behind this investor exodus, from market downturns to a shift in investor sentiment, because let's face it, nobody wants to bet on a sinking ship. We'll delve into the telltale signs that funding is drying up and how startups often find themselves on the wrong side of the financial equation. Spoiler: it's usually a recipe for chaos, with founders frantically trying to pitch their way into another round of funding while the clock ticks ominously in the background.

Through this exploration, expect to hear tales of startups that went from darlings of the venture capital world to cautionary tales in a matter of months. Think of companies that once had investors clamoring for a piece of the action but soon found themselves having to scale back, lay off employees, or even shut their doors because the cash cows ran dry. We'll examine how once-reliable funding sources become elusive mirages, and how even the most promising startups can suddenly find themselves in a financial freefall.

So grab your popcorn and settle in, because this chapter is going to be a wild ride through the highs and lows of startup funding, complete with lessons learned and warnings for those brave enough to enter the volatile world of venture capital. Get ready to uncover the harsh realities of what happens when the money stops flowing and the investors flee like they just heard the fire alarm ringing!

The Importance of Continuous Funding

The *importance of continuous funding*—the art of keeping the lights on, the champagne flowing, and that luxury car parked out front while simultaneously maintaining the façade of a successful venture. Let's be honest: continuous funding isn't just a financial necessity; it's a strategic tool for keeping the illusion alive that your startup is thriving in the cutthroat world of entrepreneurship. You know what they say: "fake it till you make it," and continuous funding is the fuel for that elaborate charade.

Picture this: you're a founder living your best life—lavish parties, luxury retreats, and that snazzy office with the bean bags and foosball tables. All of this needs to be financed, and where does that cash come from? You guessed it—continuous funding! It's like a never-ending game of Monopoly, except instead of "Go," you're just collecting investor checks. You need that funding to keep the buzz going, to maintain the illusion that your startup is the hottest thing since sliced bread.

But here's the kicker: in order to keep attracting that sweet, sweet capital, you have to create a narrative that makes it seem like you're on the path to unicorn status, even if your reality is more like a donkey with a party hat. This means discounting your product or service to entice customers, which temporarily inflates your user base but also gives the impression that you're a market leader. Who needs profitability when you can flaunt growth metrics that make it look like you're conquering the world?

Take **Groupon**, for example. They became masters of discounting to drive customer acquisition. Sure, they had millions of users, but those users were often just chasing deals rather than brand loyalty. When the discounts ended, so did the customers, and the company found itself in a world of hurt. But hey, as long as the press was buzzing about "explosive growth" and "disrupting the market," who cared about the underlying financials? They played the game beautifully until the illusion shattered.

This need for continuous funding also means investing heavily in PR campaigns to keep the hype machine running. You've got to stay in the news, showcasing your latest "innovations," partnerships, or even your founder's recent jaunt to Bali for a "retreat." PR is not just a marketing strategy; it's your lifeline to maintain that inflated valuation. You've got to convince investors and the public that you're the next big thing, even if your business model resembles a house of cards.

WeWork is a perfect case study here. They perfected the art of PR while building a narrative around community and shared workspaces. They painted themselves as the new face of work culture, but behind the scenes, their financials were a train wreck. They attracted billions in funding, all while hosting lavish parties, splurging on luxury office spaces, and throwing around buzzwords like "community" and "innovation." But when the curtains were drawn, and they filed for an IPO, the truth was far from glamorous. Investors saw the reality: a company bleeding cash while living large, and the valuation plummeted faster than a lead balloon.

In essence, continuous funding allows founders to indulge in the luxurious lifestyle that comes with the title, even when the underlying business isn't quite up to par. But remember, this is a double-edged sword. Eventually, investors will wise up to the fact that the story doesn't match the numbers, and when that day comes, the funding can dry up faster than a desert oasis.

So, if you're a founder trying to juggle discounting, a luxurious lifestyle, and the need for continuous funding, be aware that the illusion can only hold for so long. At some point, the smoke and mirrors will fade, and you'll be left with the harsh reality of what your business actually is—unless, of course, you manage to keep the funding flowing while riding that PR wave. Just remember: in the world of startups, the buzz is everything, but when the buzz fades, so might your funding.

Signs of Investor Fatigue

The moment when your once-devoted, starry-eyed investors start yawning at your pitch deck and your phone calls go straight to voicemail. It's not a question of *if* investor fatigue will hit; it's *when*. Because let's face it, even the most charismatic founder with the coolest mission statement can't dodge reality forever.

The first sign? Investors start questioning things they didn't before. Suddenly, they're asking *real* questions like, "Where's the profitability?" or "What's your actual path to sustainability?" When your investor, who previously couldn't stop talking about your unicorn status, starts sending passive-aggressive emails asking about financials, you know the fatigue is setting in. They've heard your grand vision a million times—now they want to know if you can deliver anything other than buzzwords.

Take **Theranos**, for instance. Elizabeth Holmes was the poster child for the cult of the founder, and she managed to keep investors hooked for years with slick storytelling and black turtlenecks. But when those investors started poking around the edges of the company, demanding evidence of those world-changing blood tests she promised, well... we all know how that story ended. Those early warning signs were all there—persistent questions, increasing skepticism, and a growing impatience for actual results—but the investors, swept up in the hype, ignored them for far too long. Until, of course, they couldn't.

Another big red flag is when investors stop showing up for the fun stuff—launch parties, conferences, or even casual coffee catch-ups. Back in the good ol' days of *Series A*, they'd be at every event, nodding along to your keynote speeches about "disrupting" this and "innovating" that. But now? Their calendar's suddenly full, and your invites get met with a polite, "Sorry, can't make it this time." They've moved from VIP guests to ghosting you faster than a bad Tinder date.

Uber during its wild early years is another prime example. Investors were all in, loving the crazy growth trajectory, and willing to turn a blind eye to the questionable ethics, corporate culture, and those pesky, sky-high losses. But as the scandals piled up and the company's path to profitability seemed increasingly elusive, investor fatigue set in. People started whispering, "Can this actually make money?" and when the IPO didn't deliver the payday everyone was hoping for, those whispers turned into grumbling.

Then, of course, there's the final nail in the coffin: when your investors stop reinvesting. This is when the smoke and mirrors have lost their magic. When you go back to them for more cash, and instead of that eager, "Here, take my money!" you get awkward silences or worse—some vague feedback like, "We think it's time for you to explore other funding options." Translation: "We're done pouring money into this bottomless pit." If you're at this stage, it's like realizing the party's over but you're still trying to keep the music going.

Look no further than **Juicero**, the company that famously sold a $400 juice machine that squeezed juice from pre-packaged bags of fruits and vegetables. Investors initially loved the sleek branding and Silicon Valley vibes, but as sales fizzled and people realized they could squeeze the bags *by hand*, investors started backing away, pretending they had nothing to do with it. Fatigue hit hard, and the company folded faster than you could say "cold-pressed."

In short, investor fatigue is what happens when the shine wears off, the hype dwindles, and your investors realize they've been cheering for the emperor's new clothes. It's not personal; it's just business. When those once-enthusiastic backers start getting quiet, skeptical, or outright dodging you, it's a sign that their patience—and their funds—are running on fumes. At that point, it's time to face the music and figure out if there's more to your business than just a good story.

Consequences of Funding Dry-Up

When the funding starts to dry up, the consequences can be as brutal as a hangover after a weekend bender. You might feel invincible at first, but once the adrenaline wears off, you'll be left grappling with the harsh realities of startup life. Let's break down what happens when the cash flow begins to dwindle, and your previously robust investor support is nowhere to be found.

First off, there's the gut-wrenching moment when you realize that you're not just running out of cash; you're running out of options. You thought you were the next big thing, right? But suddenly, your runway is shorter than your favorite pair of skinny jeans after a big meal. Without fresh capital, the dream of scaling quickly gets replaced with a more urgent need to cut costs. And let's be honest, nobody wants to be the founder announcing layoffs. Just ask **Zynga**, which went through multiple rounds of layoffs as their once-thriving gaming empire started to crumble under the weight of dwindling revenues and investor confidence. Those painful conversations became a regular part of the company culture, and morale took a nosedive.

Now, don't forget about the toll on your company's reputation. Investors talk, and if word gets out that you're struggling to secure funding, it's like a bad Yelp review for your startup. Suddenly, everyone from potential employees to partners to customers starts looking at you like you're carrying a red flag. Just look at **WeWork**, which went from being the golden child of the startup world to a cautionary tale after its IPO disaster. Investors pulled back faster than you can say "overvaluation," and it turned into a race to the bottom for credibility. Companies that once lined up to partner with WeWork started thinking twice, fearing their association with a sinking ship would weigh them down, too.

Then there's the frantic scramble to secure funding. You might find yourself resorting to the dreaded *friends and family round*—you know, that thing you promised yourself you'd never do. And let's be real, there's nothing quite like calling up your aunt to ask if she can lend you some cash to keep the lights on. It's embarrassing, it's stressful, and it often leads to awkward Thanksgiving dinners filled with passive-aggressive comments about your "failing venture." You might as well just wear a T-shirt that says, "I'm financially irresponsible," while you're at it.

Another delightful consequence of funding dry-up is the *scramble for survival*. You're now in the position of having to prioritize your spending, which often leads to the very essence of your startup being compromised. Strategic initiatives get sidelined, marketing budgets get slashed, and your ambitious growth plans transform into a sad little to-do list filled with "cut costs" and "survive another month." Remember **Quibi**? The short-form video platform launched with a splash but quickly found itself drowning in debt and low subscriber numbers. When they couldn't secure further funding to revamp their strategy, they were forced to shut down less than a year after launching. It was like watching a movie that promised so much but ended with a plot twist no one saw coming.

And let's not ignore the emotional rollercoaster. The pressure weighs heavily on the shoulders of founders and their teams. As funding dries up, so do the hopes and dreams. Every day feels like a ticking time bomb, and the anxiety can be palpable. This stress often leads to burnout, which is all fun and games until your team starts dropping like flies. **Better.com** saw this firsthand when it went through mass layoffs during the pandemic. The founder's approach—sending mass emails announcing layoffs—didn't exactly endear him to employees, leading to a backlash and a major hit to company culture.

Last but not least, the dry-up can lead to desperation, and that's when things get really messy. When you're starving for cash, you might consider *creative financing options*—the kind that make your lawyer sweat bullets. Think predatory loans, selling off equity at bargain-basement prices, or even worse, creating a toxic work environment to squeeze every last ounce of productivity out of your team. Just ask **Theranos**, which, in its desperate quest to keep the lights on, resorted to misleading investors and regulators about its technology and capabilities. Spoiler alert: it didn't end well.

In conclusion, the consequences of funding drying up are often severe and multi-faceted. It's not just a matter of numbers on a balance sheet; it affects company culture, reputation, team morale, and ultimately, the very future of the startup. When investors start pulling away, it's a wake-up call that demands serious introspection, adaptation, and perhaps a reality check on what it truly means to build a sustainable business. Because let's face it, in the world of startups, no funding often translates to no future.

Strategies for Securing Additional Capital

When the cash flow starts to dwindle and the investor exodus becomes a reality, founders often scramble to secure additional capital to maintain the illusion of success. It's like trying to patch a sinking ship with bubblegum; it might hold for a while, but it's only a matter of time before the reality of the situation becomes unavoidable. Let's dive into the strategies these founders employ, often with a heavy dose of sarcasm, wit, and real-world examples to keep things lively.

1. Revising the Valuation Narrative

First things first: it's time to put on that PR hat and start spinning a narrative that showcases your startup as a must-have investment. Founders often revert to a classic strategy: emphasizing their "potential" rather than their current situation. This might include inflating the growth metrics or, at the very least, carefully selecting data points that make them look more appealing than they actually are. "Sure, we may not be profitable, but did you see our user growth? We're basically the next unicorn, just without the glitter!"

Remember **Blue Apron**? After going public, they faced harsh realities, including declining subscriber numbers and increased competition. To maintain investor interest, they worked overtime to craft narratives around their supposed market potential, touting their "innovative meal kits" while conveniently glossing over their financial struggles. Spoiler alert: the narrative didn't save them, and their stock prices plummeted.

2. Desperate Discounting and Promotions

What's a founder to do when the funding is running low? Discounting to the rescue! It's like a fire sale at your local thrift store—everything must go! Founders will often resort to aggressive discounting strategies to keep customer acquisition numbers looking shiny and bright. "Look! Our user base is growing! Just ignore the fact that we're practically giving our product away."

Take **Groupon**, for instance. They became famous for their steep discounts to attract customers and maintain user engagement. However, this strategy backfired as their business model hinged on constant discounting, leading to unsustainable profits and dwindling customer loyalty. What started as a "great deal" quickly turned into a "great disaster."

3. Reaching Out to Existing Investors

Founders often go running back to their existing investors like a child looking for their parent after a bad breakup. "Please, we need more money to keep up appearances!" The hope here is that their existing backers will throw in more cash to maintain the facade of success.

They'll package their request with a bow, promising "exponential growth" and "future profitability," even if the truth is closer to "we're just trying to keep the lights on."

WeWork did this dance beautifully. After their disastrous IPO attempt, they begged their investors for a bailout, pitching it as an opportunity to right the ship. SoftBank swooped in, but it was a band-aid on a gaping wound that ultimately couldn't hide the reality of their unsustainable business model.

4. Revising the Pitch Deck

Ah, the pitch deck—the holy grail of startup storytelling. Founders often revamp their pitch decks to create a glitzy narrative that highlights growth potential and market opportunities while hiding the ugly truths. They'll throw in some fancy graphics, highlight user growth, and even add a few testimonials that could convince a houseplant to invest. "Look how great we are! You'd be a fool to miss out!"

Just look at **Theranos**, whose founders curated their pitch deck to create an image of revolutionary technology and untapped potential. They lured in investors with promises of transforming healthcare, all while hiding the fact that their product didn't even work. When the truth came out, it was a masterclass in how not to secure capital—because, spoiler alert, you can't build a company on lies.

5. Seeking Out New Investors with a Fresh Spin

When all else fails, it's time to broaden the horizon and seek out new investors. Founders often put on a brave face and hit the streets, looking for new backers who haven't been exposed to their current financial woes. They might attempt to sell their startup as the latest and greatest opportunity, emphasizing how undervalued they are compared to the competition. "You can get in on the ground floor of the next big thing! What's a little cash for potential greatness?"

Look at **Kraft Heinz**. They faced intense scrutiny and public criticism due to stagnant growth and profitability concerns. Yet, instead of acknowledging their struggles, they aggressively pursued new partnerships and investors, trying to convince them that they were still the household name everyone wanted. Spoiler: It didn't work out as planned, and their struggles continued.

6. Leveraging Strategic Partnerships

Founders might also pivot towards forming strategic partnerships with other businesses as a means of securing capital. "Let's team up with someone who has a better reputation and more cash flow! It'll make us look good and maybe even provide some much-needed funds." This can be a double-edged sword, though—if the partnership goes south, it can bring down both parties.

Remember **Sears**? Once a retail giant, they formed partnerships with other brands to boost sales and bring in more customers. However, these partnerships often lacked synergy, leaving Sears with more issues than solutions. The company ended up teetering on the brink of bankruptcy, proving that sometimes two wrongs don't make a right—especially in the business world.

Conclusion

In the grand scheme of things, when the funding starts to dry up, founders resort to a mix of creativity, desperation, and occasionally sheer delusion to secure additional capital. It's a wild ride filled with discounting, narrative-spinning, and partnership-seeking, all while keeping up the pretense of success. But as history has shown us time and again, you can only keep the charade going for so long before reality comes crashing down like a poorly constructed house of cards. So, to all the founders out there: good luck, and remember, it's a thin line between genius and lunacy in the world of startups!

Resilience in the Face of Funding Challenges

Navigating the treacherous waters of startup funding is a test of resilience, and oh boy, does it take a special kind of determination to keep afloat when the sharks are circling. Picture this: you're in a small boat on a vast ocean, and suddenly, a storm hits. You can either throw your hands up and surrender to the waves or grab the oars and start rowing like your life depends on it—which, in the world of startups, it often does.

Take **Airbnb**, for instance. In the early days, when they were struggling to secure funding, they resorted to some creative solutions to stay alive. When the 2008 financial crisis hit, they faced the reality that their business model was shaky at best. Instead of throwing in the towel, the founders—Brian Chesky, Joe Gebbia, and Nathan Blecharczyk—took a different approach. They sold cereal boxes labeled "Obama O's" and "Cap'n McCain" during the presidential election to raise a quick $30,000. It was a brilliant marketing stunt that not only generated cash but also drew attention to their platform. That kind of ingenuity and determination exemplifies resilience. They weren't just weathering the storm; they were figuring out how to make it work for them.

Then there's **Slack**, which started as a gaming company called Tiny Speck. After its game failed to take off, rather than admitting defeat and walking away, the founders pivoted to the internal communication tool that became Slack. They didn't just fold; they adapted, learned from their mistakes, and turned a setback into a billion-dollar idea. The ability to pivot and recognize when something isn't working is the hallmark of resilient entrepreneurs. They didn't cling to their original vision like a lifeline; they let it go and set sail for new horizons.

We can also look at **Groupon**, which, after its initial success, faced significant challenges with profitability and competition. Instead of shutting down, they made bold moves, including layoffs and restructuring, to adapt to their new reality. While their approach was often criticized, it's worth noting that they kept pushing forward, desperately trying to find a sustainable business model. The thing is, in the world of startups, resilience sometimes means making tough decisions that may not be popular but are necessary for survival.

The founders of **Zocdoc** encountered their own set of obstacles, particularly during the initial years when they struggled to gain traction. As they faced skepticism from investors about their viability, the team doubled down on their mission. They spent countless hours listening to users, refining their product, and ensuring that they were addressing real pain points in the healthcare system. Their commitment to resilience paid off when they eventually secured funding, enabling them to expand their services significantly. They exemplified the notion that sometimes the most resilient entrepreneurs are those who are willing to listen, learn, and evolve, even when the odds are stacked against them.

And then we have **Kiva**, the micro-lending platform that started out with an ambitious mission: to connect people through lending for poverty alleviation. In the early days, securing enough funding and support was a struggle. But instead of giving up, the founders sought out passionate individuals and grassroots movements to help them build a community around their mission. Through persistent outreach, they eventually gained traction and expanded their network of lenders. Their story is a testament to resilience; they turned what could have been a failed idea into a thriving platform by engaging with people who shared their vision.

Resilience in the face of funding challenges is often about maintaining the right mindset. It's about understanding that failure is not the end; it's just a part of the journey. **Spotify** faced its own challenges when negotiating licensing deals with music labels. The road was bumpy, filled with rejections and demands that felt insurmountable. Yet, instead of succumbing to despair, they held their ground, persisted in negotiations, and eventually built a platform that transformed the music industry. Their resilience wasn't just about bouncing back; it was about believing in their vision enough to weather the storms of skepticism and doubt.

To wrap it all up, resilience in the startup world is less about invincibility and more about adaptability. It's the art of standing back up after getting knocked down and figuring out how to make the next move work. Whether it's through creative fundraising methods, hard pivots, or simply refusing to give in to the noise of negativity, the most successful entrepreneurs are those who learn to embrace the challenges and keep pushing forward, even when the going gets tough. After all, in the chaotic world of startups, every obstacle can be a stepping stone to greatness—if only you have the resilience to leap over it!

The Future of Startups: Is There a Way Out?

As we reach the final chapter of this rollercoaster ride through the wild world of startups, it's time to lift the veil and ask the burning question on everyone's mind: Is there a way out of this quagmire? We've navigated through inflated valuations, the cult of the founder, and the customer acquisition trap, and now we're left with the remnants of what was once a glittering dream. But don't despair! Just like a phoenix rising from the ashes, there's hope for a more sustainable future in the startup ecosystem.

In this chapter, we'll dive into the evolving landscape of startups—examining trends that could lead to a healthier and more grounded approach to entrepreneurship. We'll explore how founders can ditch the shiny unicorn myth and embrace a more pragmatic mindset that values profitability over perpetual growth. Yes, I said it—profitability! Shocking, right? We'll look at companies that have chosen to put down the fairy dust and focus on real, tangible results rather than chasing that elusive billion-dollar valuation.

But hold onto your hats, because we'll also discuss the role of investors in this new era. Can they be the change-makers we need, or will they continue to fuel the chaos? We'll take a peek at what happens when investors finally wake up from their slumber, realizing that it's not just about the next big exit but about building resilient companies that can weather the storms of economic uncertainty.

We'll explore how innovation doesn't always have to mean creating the next flashy app or tech product. Sometimes, it's about refining existing models, understanding customer needs, and creating value in ways that matter—like taking care of the environment, enhancing community engagement, and addressing real-world issues. Sounds revolutionary, doesn't it?

And let's not forget about the potential for a cultural shift in how we view startups. It's high time we redefined success—not just in terms of growth and valuation but also through the lens of sustainability and social responsibility. Who knew that being a successful startup could also mean being a good citizen?

So, buckle up as we embark on this exploration of the future of startups. Together, we'll chart a course toward a landscape where the focus shifts from inflated dreams to realistic goals, where the hustle doesn't overshadow health, and where success isn't measured just by dollars and cents, but by impact and integrity. Ready or not, the future is here, and it's time to make it a better one!

Is the Unicorn Model Dead?

The unicorn model isn't exactly dead, but it's definitely wheezing and gasping for air—like that poor fish you found flopping around on the beach, desperately trying to find its way back to the water. Sure, we still have those rare billion-dollar startups that capture everyone's attention and make the headlines, but the shiny allure of being a "unicorn" is starting to lose its luster.

In the past, being a unicorn was like winning the lottery: everyone wanted in on the action. Founders, investors, and the media alike all played their roles in perpetuating this myth of boundless growth and instant success. The model thrived on a cocktail of inflated valuations, aggressive growth strategies, and a healthy dose of hype. But as we've seen, this ride often ends in a spectacular crash—hello, WeWork, and bon voyage, Rivian!

The shift is largely due to several factors. First off, the market is maturing (read: sobering up) after years of wild speculation. Investors are now asking the hard questions: "Where's the profit?" and "What's your path to sustainability?" It's like that moment when you wake up from a night of partying and realize your bank account is almost empty—suddenly, the glittery allure of that cocktail doesn't seem so enticing anymore.

Moreover, a growing number of founders are waking up to the realization that growth at all costs isn't a viable long-term strategy. They're prioritizing sustainable practices over relentless expansion, which means they're less likely to chase that elusive unicorn status. Take companies like Basecamp, for example. They've built their success on a foundation of profitability and thoughtful growth, making it clear that you don't need to be a unicorn to thrive.

Investors, too, are beginning to pivot away from the unicorn model. Many are now looking for businesses that can demonstrate real value, profitability, and the ability to weather economic storms. This shift might just be the slap of reality that the startup ecosystem desperately needed.

In short, while the unicorn model isn't completely extinct, it's definitely in a state of decline. As the startup world evolves, we may find ourselves in an era where "horse" is the new unicorn—more reliable, sustainable, and grounded in reality. The fairy tales of fast riches and instant success are giving way to stories of resilience, adaptability, and the pursuit of meaningful impact. So, let's raise a glass to the unicorns—but not too high; we wouldn't want to shatter the fragile illusion!

So, if the unicorn model is taking a backseat, what can we learn from this shift? It's time to ditch the fairy tale fantasies and get down to the nitty-gritty of building a solid business. Here are some principles and tips to help you create a sustainable venture that doesn't just rely on buzz and hype:

1. Prioritize Profitability Over Hype: The allure of massive funding rounds and sky-high valuations can be intoxicating, but at the end of the day, cash flow is king. Focus on building a business that can sustain itself financially. This means understanding your costs, setting realistic pricing, and knowing your market. For instance, consider **ProfitWell**, a SaaS company that focuses on subscription metrics and pricing strategies. They prioritize revenue retention and profitability, which has led to steady growth without needing to chase down endless rounds of funding.

2. Build a Solid Product-Market Fit: Forget about the shiny marketing campaigns for a second and focus on what truly matters: your customers. Your product should solve a real problem for a specific audience. Conduct thorough market research and gather feedback to iterate your offering. Look at **Dropbox**—they started with a simple product and a killer referral program that tapped directly into user needs, allowing them to grow organically rather than relying solely on investor hype.

3. Embrace Transparency and Authenticity: In a world filled with smoke and mirrors, honesty is refreshing. Build trust with your customers and investors by being transparent about your business operations and financial health. **Buffer**, a social media management tool, has built a loyal user base by openly sharing their revenue, employee salaries, and even their challenges. This authenticity not only strengthens relationships but also sets a precedent for accountability.

4. Develop a Resilient Business Model: Relying on a single revenue stream or chasing trends is a recipe for disaster. Diversify your offerings and explore multiple income sources. For example, **Airbnb** started as a platform for short-term rentals but expanded into experiences and other travel-related services, allowing them to weather market fluctuations. This adaptability can make your business more resilient in the face of economic changes.

5. Invest in Customer Relationships: Rather than focusing solely on acquisition through discounts and promotions, prioritize long-term relationships with your customers. A loyal customer base is far more valuable than a temporary influx of sales. Look at **Zappos**—their legendary customer service has turned one-time buyers into lifelong advocates. By focusing on delivering value and creating positive experiences, you'll cultivate a community that supports your growth.

6. Foster a Strong Company Culture: Your team is the backbone of your business. A toxic culture can drive talent away and undermine your mission. Build an inclusive and supportive environment where employees feel valued and motivated to contribute. Companies like **Patagonia** prioritize environmental and social responsibility while empowering their employees, leading to higher engagement and retention.

7. Set Realistic Growth Goals: Dream big, but keep your feet on the ground. Rapid growth isn't always sustainable, and overextending yourself can lead to disaster. Establish realistic milestones that align with your financial capabilities and market conditions. **Mailchimp**, for instance, grew steadily and avoided external funding until they were ready to scale. This cautious approach allowed them to maintain control and profitability.

8. Embrace Feedback and Iteration: The startup journey is not a straight line; it's a series of twists, turns, and occasional detours. Be open to feedback from customers, employees, and even investors. Use this input to iterate your product, refine your strategies, and pivot when necessary. Companies like **Slack** started as a gaming company but pivoted to a communication tool based on user feedback. This flexibility is key to staying relevant and resilient.

In conclusion, the future of startups lies not in chasing the elusive unicorn status but in building real businesses grounded in principles of sustainability, profitability, and customer loyalty. By embracing these tips, you'll cultivate a venture that can thrive in the long run, weathering the storms of the market while avoiding the pitfalls of hype and superficial success. After all, the goal isn't just to be the loudest voice in the room—it's to build a lasting legacy that resonates with customers and investors alike. So let's turn off the smoke machine, put away the mirrors, and get to work!

How Stakeholders Can Push for Change

If there's one group that can actually steer this runaway unicorn, it's the stakeholders—the people who either have skin in the game or just a vested interest in seeing these companies not crash and burn. And trust me, it's in everyone's best interest to not keep investing in fantasies. So, how do they push for real, sustainable change instead of chasing a mythical beast?

Let's start with investors. These are the people who are literally pouring gasoline on the fire or, if they're smart, can start cooling it down. They have one thing that startups need to survive: money. And guess what? They can choose to *not* throw it at companies that are all sizzle and no steak. If investors stop blindly funding the next "disruptor" that has no actual plan to be profitable, they could actually force startups to—get this—focus on building a real business. I mean, shocking, right? You want your millions to go somewhere? How about demanding actual results, like a path to profitability, not just endless growth and a few good PR stunts?

And it's not just about throwing cash around. Investors can also use their positions to push for changes at the governance level. A good example is Engine No. 1, a hedge fund that shook up ExxonMobil, pushing for greener policies. If that's possible in a century-old oil giant, imagine what can be done in startups if investors collectively decide to push for long-term sustainability over the flashy, short-term buzz.

Employees also hold more power than they realize. They're the ones in the trenches, building the product, sweating over deadlines, and ultimately making the vision (or delusion) come to life. But what happens when they start realizing they're just part of a hype machine? We've seen walkouts, strikes, and even internal memos that challenge company leadership. And when enough people push back—saying, "Hey, maybe we should stop burning millions just to acquire users who will vanish as soon as we stop giving them discounts"—that's when the foundation shakes. Because a company isn't anything without the people doing the actual work.

Now, let's talk customers. They're not just passive participants. Consumers are becoming more savvy, and in the era of conscious spending, many now want to see companies that align with their values. Sure, people love a discount. But more and more, we're seeing a shift toward supporting businesses that are transparent, sustainable, and focused on real value rather than just the next "unicorn" status. Companies can only burn cash on discounts and fake growth for so long before customers catch on that it's a house of cards.

Finally, there's a role for regulatory bodies, even though that's not the sexiest thing to talk about. But let's be real: some of these companies would never have gotten this far without a little light oversight—or rather, a complete lack of it. A few more rules around transparency, accountability, and financial disclosures could go a long way in preventing another Theranos-level disaster. Nobody likes more regulation, but sometimes you need to step in when founders are off playing the hype game while the ship's on fire.

At the end of the day, the unicorn model doesn't have to be dead. But it does need a major reality check. Building a solid business isn't just about scaling fast, getting featured in *Forbes*, and crossing that billion-dollar valuation line. It's about making something that lasts, something that provides real value, not just smoke and mirrors. And if stakeholders—all of them—start pushing for that kind of change, we might actually see fewer unicorns... and more real, sustainable businesses. And wouldn't that be something?

The Role of Investors in a Healthier Ecosystem

Let's talk about investors—the puppet masters behind the scenes of every startup circus. In the unhealthy ecosystem we've built, they're the ones fanning the flames of wild valuations, demanding exponential growth while ignoring profits, and handing out money like it's candy at Halloween. But what if they decided to flip the script and actually create a healthier startup ecosystem? Yeah, I know—sounds crazy, right? But it's possible.

Take *Benchmark Capital* as an example. These guys were early investors in *Uber*, and while they rode the wild ride that Uber was, they were also one of the first to call out its toxicity. When the founder and CEO, Travis Kalanick, was steering the ship straight into a PR and ethical disaster, Benchmark didn't sit idly by. They *forced* him out. Sure, it was a messy affair, but it shows that investors can push for the right kind of leadership when things start going off the rails. If more investors had this level of backbone, maybe we'd see fewer companies run by egomaniacal founders and more businesses with actual sustainable practices.

Then there's the case of *Sequoia Capital*. They've had their hands in a ton of successful startups, but they're not just throwing money around. When they invested in *WhatsApp*, they didn't push for wild growth at any cost. They invested in a company that had a lean team, focused on real value—building a messaging platform people actually used and *loved*. When Facebook came knocking with $19 billion, they cashed out, sure, but the point is Sequoia didn't demand that WhatsApp burn through cash just to acquire users with fake growth metrics. They invested in a solid product with a real, clear business model, and that made all the difference.

On the flip side, let's not forget the disaster that was *WeWork*. Investors, including SoftBank's Vision Fund, pumped billions into the company, enabling Adam Neumann to create what was essentially a real estate company masquerading as a tech startup. Neumann had free reign to spend lavishly, fly private jets, and make outlandish claims about the future of work—all while the business was hemorrhaging money. When it came time to go public, the reality of WeWork's broken business model came crashing down. Investors had enabled the hype and fantasy for far too long, and when the bubble burst, they paid the price.

What we can learn from these examples is that investors have the power to shape the trajectory of a startup—for better or worse. They can fuel unhealthy growth obsessions (like with WeWork), or they can take a stand and push for healthy, sustainable business practices (as Benchmark did with Uber). Imagine if more investors followed the Sequoia WhatsApp model: prioritizing products that actually have a path to profitability, rather than chasing the next billion-dollar valuation based on nothing but buzzwords and fake metrics.

It's also worth looking at *Y Combinator*, one of the most famous startup accelerators. They've funded hundreds of companies, but what's interesting is their focus on long-term thinking. *Sam Altman*, a former president of YC, has been outspoken about how important it is to back founders who are building real businesses, not just chasing the next round of funding. Companies like *Airbnb* and *Stripe* came out of Y Combinator, and while they grew quickly, they were always anchored in solid business models. Airbnb, for instance, wasn't about explosive, unsustainable user growth at first—it was about creating a trusted community. The growth came because people liked the product, not because they were getting endless discounts or investors were pushing them to burn cash.

What would happen if more investors pushed for this kind of mentality? Instead of demanding startups show hockey-stick growth graphs and billion-dollar valuations after Series A, they could focus on real business fundamentals: profitability, customer retention, and actual value creation. Investors have the money, the influence, and the power to demand better—and if they do, we'd see fewer startups crash and burn after reaching "unicorn" status.

Ultimately, investors need to step up. They can't keep throwing money at every new startup that comes out of Silicon Valley with a flashy pitch deck. They need to ask the tough questions: How are you going to make money? When will you be profitable? Are you building something that people will still care about in five years, or are you just chasing the next PR headline? If investors start holding startups to higher standards, we might finally break free from the current cycle of hype and failure, and start building a startup ecosystem that's actually sustainable.

In short: more accountability, less unicorn chasing.

End Note: Vision for a Sustainable Startup Future

The startup world needs a serious reality check. We've spent way too long chasing unicorns—those mythical billion-dollar valuations built on hype, buzz, and the faint hope that one day, somehow, the cash-burning furnace of growth will magically turn into a profit machine. Spoiler alert: it won't.

My vision for a sustainable startup future? Simple. Let's ditch the obsession with hype and start focusing on the fundamentals—*real* businesses, serving *real* customers, with actual *value* to offer. Yeah, I know, sounds boring compared to the latest unicorn fantasy where a company with no revenue is worth $10 billion, but hear me out.

First things first: **profitability is not a dirty word.** Too often, founders are led to believe that profits are some far-off goal to be worried about later. Later never comes. Instead of chasing exponential growth from day one, we should be encouraging startups to focus on building something profitable—no more "we'll figure it out once we're big enough" nonsense. Build something that makes money *now*, not when you're the next Amazon. If you're not solving a real problem that people are willing to pay for, then why are you even in business?

Next, **we need to stop rewarding toxic hustle culture.** The "work 20 hours a day, burn yourself out, grind until you die" mentality is broken. It's time to admit that the so-called hustle culture is just a fancy term for burnout. A sustainable startup future means prioritizing the well-being of founders and employees alike. You can't build a lasting business if everyone is too exhausted to think straight.

Then there's **the founder cult problem**—this whole idolization of founders has to go. We put these people on pedestals and act like they're gods among men just because they've secured some VC funding. Guess what? Raising money doesn't mean you're building a great business. It just means you're good at pitching. It's time we stop worshipping the idea of the "visionary founder" and start focusing on the teams that actually make the company run. The real heroes of startups are the employees grinding it out behind the scenes, not just the founder posting motivational quotes on Twitter.

Investors, you're up next. You need to change the game. Stop throwing billions at startups that have no path to profitability, just because they make a lot of noise. You have the power to set the standards. Instead of looking for the next headline-grabbing unicorn, why not invest in companies that are sustainable from the get-go? Push founders to build solid, profitable businesses, not just vanity metrics. You should be demanding more from your investments than just user growth and buzz.

Customers also play a huge role in this vision. Stop chasing discounts and free services just because they're dangled in front of you like shiny objects. Support businesses that offer real value and charge for it fairly. This endless cycle of discount-driven customer acquisition is driving startups to the ground. Businesses need to make money, and that means customers need to be willing to pay for quality products and services.

Finally, **startups themselves need to embrace transparency**. No more smoke and mirrors. Be upfront about where you are, what you're doing, and how you're going to get there. If you're burning cash, say it. If you're struggling to find a path to profitability, own it. But work toward fixing it instead of pretending everything's fine while the ship is sinking. Honesty with investors, employees, and customers is what will separate the flash-in-the-pan startups from those that are built to last.

In a sustainable startup future, **buzz takes a back seat to business fundamentals**. Founders are celebrated for creating real value, not just for raising capital. Investors are praised for backing solid companies, not just the latest hype machine. And customers? They're not just along for the ride—they're the ones driving the change by supporting businesses that actually care about long-term sustainability.

It's time to end the unicorn fantasy and get back to the basics. Startups can be exciting, innovative, and world-changing—but they need to be grounded in reality. That's the future I'm betting on, and it's one where sustainable, profitable businesses outlast the hype. So, here's to killing the unicorn myth and building something that actually matters.

www.ingramcontent.com/pod-product-compliance
Lightning Source LLC
Chambersburg PA
CBHW052144220526
45471CB00004B/1515